JEWELRY

DESIGN

THE ARTISAN'S REFERENCE

ELIZABETH OLVER

NORTH LIGHT BOOKS
Cincinnati, Ohio

A QUARTO BOOK

First published in North America
in 2000 by North Light Books,
an imprint of F&W Publications, Inc.,
1507 Dana Avenue
Cincinnati, OH 45207
1-800/289-0963

ISBN 1-58180-094-0

QUAR.JDSF

Conceived, designed and produced by
Quarto Publishing plc
The Old Brewery
6 Blundell Street
London N7 9BH

Editor Steffanie Diamond Brown
Art Editor & Designer Sheila Volpe
Assistant Art Director Penny Cobb
Illustrators Neville Morgan,
Amina Bolton, Elizabeth Olver
Copy Editor Ian Kearey
Picture Researcher Laurent Boubounelle
Proofreader Neil Cole
Indexer Dorothy Frame

Art Director Moira Clinch
Publisher Piers Spence

Manufactured by Regent Publishing
Services Ltd, Hong Kong.
Printed by Leefung-Asco Printers, China.

The author and publisher can accept no
liability for the use or misuse of any
materials mentioned in this book. Always
read all product and equipment labels, and
take all necessary precautions.

CONTENTS

My personal interest in jewelry started very early in my life, and could almost be said to have been a natural affinity. Like a magpie, I have always been drawn to objects that sparkle. As a child, I couldn't resist jewelry: I would feast on the forms in the window of a store, or marvel at my mother as she left for a party, beautiful in her gowns and jewels.

Since those early days, my understanding and appreciation of jewelry has evolved and grown. My first degree, from the Central School of Art in London, opened my eyes to the joy of jewelry forms, and to the satisfaction of realizing ideas through fabrication. My second degree, from the Royal College of Art in London, helped me to hone my instincts, and to develop a cognitive approach to jewelry, allowing me to appreciate and understand it in a way I had not thought possible.

Jewelry may be seen by some as a luxury, and although it would be hard to assert that it is actually a necessity, it is surprising how at times we may miss it—many people actually feel naked leaving the house without their jewelry on. A finger suddenly denuded of a long-worn ring can be a distressing experience. Jewelry can

A silver ring that interprets Noah's Ark in a jewelry format.

become almost part of our identity, and jewels can leave their mark—the naked finger will almost certainly have a "waist" where the ring has sat comfortably for years.

A COMPREHENSIVE LOOK

At first glance, jewelry appears to be a subject about which a person might confidently be able to say what sort of piece he or she might commission if offered the opportunity. Chances are that the person would consider using precious material and gemstones in order to define a form of value that was functional, and that would adorn the body. Perhaps the piece would be marked for a particular occasion, such as a Valentine's day present, a twenty-first birthday party, a graduation, or an engagement of marriage. Most people would refer to visual stimuli for inspiration for such a commission. The obvious places to look are a mainstream jewelry store, magazines, and art galleries. Even in such places, however, one would still not likely be treated to a comprehensive look at the immense range of jewelry out there, for the simple reason that it is relatively well hidden. This book is designed as a reference for those who are interested in viewing some of the treasures that we don't normally get to see—certainly not in one place and in such numbers—although it is a mere tip of the iceberg. This book also aims to provide an overview of some of the most popular jewelry forms. The great variety of shapes, colors, textures, materials, and ideas that are represented here may even act as a catalyst for the more conservative among us to consider moving away from a predictable path, and to reassess our image of jewelry. Through both illustrated and photographic images, this book shows what a broad subject area jewelry is, and how difficult the choices can be when faced with a commission.

This striking piece of enamel work uses dynamic motifs to attract our attention.

AN UNDERSTANDING OF QUALITY

For jewelry to be perfect or exemplary, it need not be fussy or showy, but it should have a sense of quality. Quality is what distinguishes a piece, and quality is the ingredient, to my mind, that makes a piece of jewelry noteworthy. Quality is partially a matter of taste, although it can be said that there is a certain subconscious expectation and understanding of the concept of quality that is common to us all. A line, for example, can be seen as being of a high quality for having just the right curve or flow; similarly, an object may beckon us to hold and covet it because of its inherent qualities—its weight and tactile surface, for example.

THE LANGUAGE OF SHAPE AND FORM

There are too many facets of a piece of jewelry to mention each one individually, but our first impression is most likely to be of its physical shape and form. The reasons why one form is more successful than another are difficult to define, although there is an instinctive sense of balance in form, even in the most inexperienced of us, that dictates its appeal. The language of shape and form could be said to be a balance of instinct and association; some forms just "feel" right, while others suggest that they are merely right for the job. We would expect a ring form to have a hole through which we could pass a finger, but we would not expect the ring walls to be too wide for us to close our other fingers around it. It is also possible to draw attention to the form of a piece by using unusual combinations of materials, colors, textures, or finishes, so that we are made to consider their appropriateness. For example, we would not expect a crab to have a leopard's pelt—and this would certainly attract attention. Similarly, a necklace with gold pendants shaped like razors might make us look twice—although the imagery is aggressive, the material disperses any feeling of threat.

There are so many ways in which jewelry can be made to excite and intrigue us. Even now, after years of immersion in jewelry and jewelry-making, I continue to delight in the fact that there is virtually no end to the permutations of form and concept that jewelry can offer. This book brings together a myriad of forms to illustrate the inherent wealth of the subject for those who are new to its delights, while confirming its breadth and depth for those of us who are already hooked.

A mokumé gane brooch featuring a classic bark-like texture.

This silver locket has a personal agenda: it holds a lock of hair.

HOW TO USE THIS BOOK

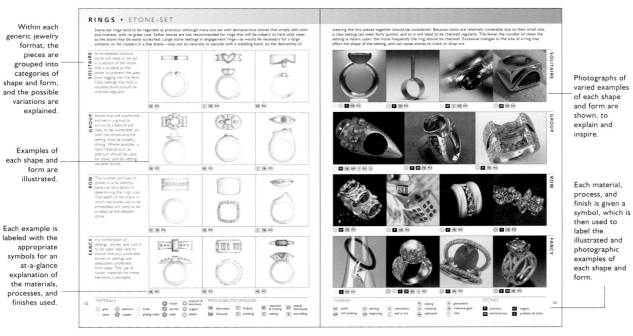

Within each generic jewelry format, the pieces are grouped into categories of shape and form, and the possible variations are explained.

Examples of each shape and form are illustrated.

Each example is labeled with the appropriate symbols for an at-a-glance explanation of the materials, processes, and finishes used.

Photographs of varied examples of each shape and form are shown, to explain and inspire.

Each material, process, and finish is given a symbol, which is then used to label the illustrated and photographic examples of each shape and form.

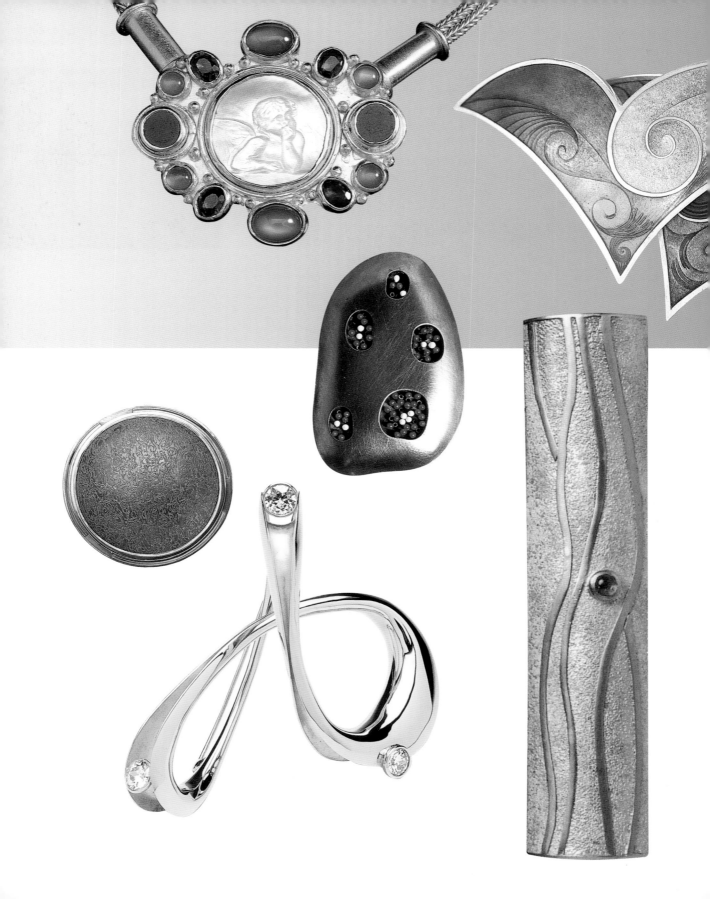

Jewelry-making is an ancient craft, and many of the techniques and materials used thousands of years ago are still used today. Rarely is a piece of jewelry constructed using only one

Techniques & Materials

technique or material. A single piece may have a cast section, a carved detail, an enamelled area, and a claw-set precious stone. Some of the most popular jewelry-making techniques and materials are described here, to give you an overview of the range of possibilities, and to inspire you to experiment on your own.

PROCESSES

While advances in metallurgy and the introduction of electrically-powered equipment have led to great improvements in many areas of jewelry-making, a surprisingly sophisticated range of jewelry can be fabricated using just a few basic tools and techniques. All of the processes outlined below are suitable for small-scale studios, with the exception of the casting process. The most commonly used casting technique for jewelry is centrifugal casting, which involves a number of expensive pieces of equipment. Because casting requires a great deal of practice for good results, and because it is an expensive process, it is advisable to use a professional company to undertake this sort of work.

BASIC FABRICATION

Fabrication using basic hand tools and bench work has hardly changed over the centuries, and a large number of jewelry shapes can still be made using these techniques. Basic jewelry skills such as piercing, filing, soldering, forming, and finishing are essential for jewelry-making, and will inevitably be involved in nearly every piece of jewelry made, even if only for finishing or basic assembly. Even a minimum use of these skills can be enough to create a complex piece of jewelry.

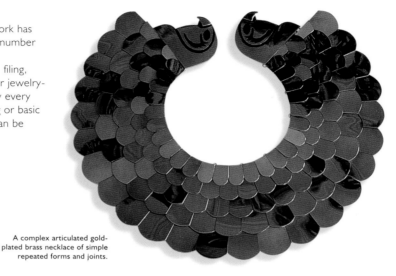

A complex articulated gold-plated brass necklace of simple repeated forms and joints.

REPOUSSÉ & CHASING

Repoussé and chasing are processes for embossing sheet metal. In chasing, steel tools are hammered into the front of the sheet's surface, while repoussé involves working the sheet from the backside. Used in combination, sheet metal can be worked to create relief and hollow forms in both positive and negative. Each mark made with a tool will result in an alteration of the sheet—the sheet is held steady in a pitch bowl, and the overall body of work flexes to compensate, allowing the metal to be displaced.

PRESSING

Pressing takes the simple principle of a doming punch and block and applies it to more sophisticated tooling to produce hollow sheet forms. The tools are made in two parts: a positive and a negative. A thin sheet of metal is placed between the two parts and then pressed, creating a skin that follows the form of the interface between the two forms. A variety of metals with a reasonable level of elasticity, including copper and gold, can be used in this way to make a repeated shape.

Repoussé and chasing are used to create delicate patinated leaf-shaped earrings.

In these three brooches, the same forms are transformed by different materials and decorative elements.

CASTING

Casting provides an opportunity to make three-dimensional forms in metal from forms that can be carved or constructed from wax, soap, or other organic materials. A hollow plaster form is filled with molten metal to cast a three-dimensional form; a rubber mold can then be made to produce additional copies. Centrifugal casting is used to make one-off pieces of jewelry, or multiple pieces using different materials. Cuttlefish- and sand-casting are more primitive techniques, and are suitable for small workshops.

A single unit is cast to create clusters of granulated pendant forms.

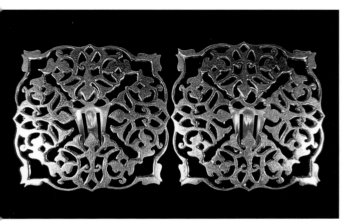

A fretwork design is repeated by casting and assembled as decorative clip earrings.

FRETWORK

Also known as piercing, in fretwork a fine jeweler's saw called a piercing saw is used to hand-saw patterns into metal. This technique can be used to transform a plain piece of sheet metal into a delicate and intricate piece of jewelry. Often, a pattern is drawn on tracing paper, and the paper is attached by double-sided tape to the metal; the metal is then pierced following the lines of the tracing. If desired, the piece can be further worked by using other processes, such as filing or hammering.

FORGING

Forging is a way of stretching, flattening, curving, and shaping metal by applying force from different directions using specially shaped hammers. The hammers are applied from above, while the metal sits on a stake or an anvil. Like so many other aspects of making jewelry, forging is about balancing strength with control, delicacy, and accuracy. At a basic level, the forging process is particularly useful for imparting character to sheet and wire with minimal manipulation.

Forged wires are joined to form a skeletal chain that is simple yet sophisticated in form.

The forging technique is used here to create a series of rings. Each ring in the series differs slightly from the others, and each represents a separate facet of the artist's exploration of form through the technique.

9

SPECIAL TECHNIQUES

Specialized techniques such as spinning and turning with a lathe can involve expensive and complex machinery that may not be readily available. These processes can be dangerous, and it is thus advisable to seek professional instruction, and to observe all health and safety procedures. Photoetching can be achieved in a suitably equipped workshop—there are also companies who will photoetch professionally. Anticlastic raising and some knit-and-weave techniques may require the use of specialized tools.

KNIT & WEAVE

Fine metal wires such as cloisonné wire can be used instead of thread for weaving and knitting. Different colors can be achieved by the use of different metals, and can be further accentuated with patination. Weaving, French knitting, crocheting, and other techniques suitable for thread can be used to make flat sheets and tubes, as well as more sculptural, three-dimensional forms.

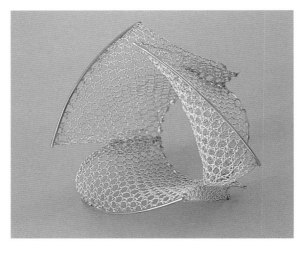

Knitted silver wire "sails" are assembled into a delicate sculptural form in this bangle.

SPINNING

Spinning is a potentially dangerous technique, and involves a great deal of sensitivity and skill. It is done on a spinning lathe; using the body's weight to push large, hand-held tools, a disk of metal is eased over a solid form. Accurate, lightweight forms based on the round can be made by spinning. The process can also be used for making hollow forms designed for assembly in two parts.

ANTICLASTIC RAISING

Anticlastic raising on sheet metal creates curvaceous, hollow forms that resemble open gullies, undulating and curving in two directions at the same point. A tapered, snaking form made of wood or steel, called a sinusoidal stake, is needed for this unusual form of forging. A wedge-shaped hammer is used to form the metal into curvaceous gully shapes.

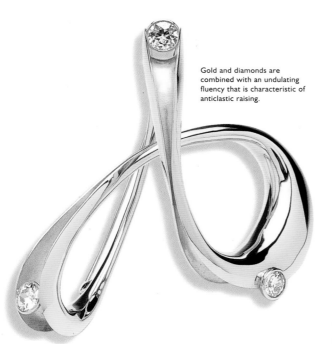

Gold and diamonds are combined with an undulating fluency that is characteristic of anticlastic raising.

Spinning is used to create a hollow form with articulated bronze details in this bold bangle.

PHOTOETCHING

In this form of etching, ultraviolet light is used to expose artwork on sensitized metal sheets that are then etched using acids to corrode the metal. Recesses can be etched to a given depth into the surface of a sheet of metal for enamelling, or to create a patterned surface, or all the way through to cut out spaces. Photoetching for jewelry is usually done by commercial firms.

Electroformed copper detail is used to create a leafy pattern on a ring carved from Perspex.

ELECTROFORMING

In this process, a skin of metal is deposited onto a form, having been transferred from a metallic anode to a form that has become a synthesized metal cathode. A lightweight, hard skin of metal then covers the form, which must be non-porous. Metal detail can be achieved by hand-painting the synthesizing solution so that the form is not entirely covered.

LATHE WORK

A lathe is a large piece of machinery used to hold forms and rotate them at high speed, allowing the material to be worked using steel tools. The lathe can be used to create very accurate work within a specific format. Relatively simple to use, small lathes can be found for making small, turned, decorative work, and for wax turning, screw threads, drilling, making jump rings, and small tooling. Larger lathes generally require professional instruction, and experience is necessary in order to use them safely and accurately.

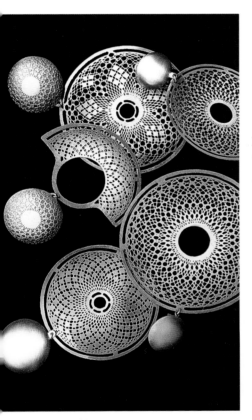

A collection of decorative photoetched jewelry forms are reminiscent of lace with their linear patterns.

A pendant form comprised of a lathe-turned horn bead set in a lathe-turned silver mount creates a feeling of antiquity.

ANODIZING

The anodizing process is used for coloring the surface of certain metals; aluminum and titanium are the two most common in the context of jewelry-making. The chemicals, preparation, and process of anodizing differ for the two types of metal, as does the intensity of the colors created—the colors are brighter in aluminum than titanium, although a wide spectrum can be achieved in both.

Colored by anodizing, the aluminum "dumbbell" features are removable, and are meant to be worn in conjunction with a square silver ring.

MATERIALS

The variety of materials used for making jewelry is constantly growing. Well-established materials such as gold and silver can be seen frequently in finished jewelry forms, while base metals such as copper, brass, gilding metal, and nickel are more commonly used for model-making and prototyping—although they are also sometimes found in finished jewelry forms. Organic materials have long been used in jewelry, while titanium and aluminum are relative newcomers, not seen as jewelry forms as often. The use of plastics for casting and embedding is also on the rise.

GOLD

Gold is the metal most commonly associated with jewelry. In its purest form, gold is very soft and inert, but modern alloying techniques now provide access to different levels of purity and malleability.

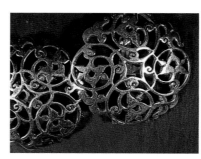

A gold ring is forged to flow fluidly, with a stamen-like tendril that culminates in a beaten gold-grained detail.

SILVER

Sterling, or standard silver, is an alloy of pure silver, and is widely used by jewelers because it is harder than fine silver and therefore more durable and suitable for jewelry. It does, however, oxidize more readily.

Silver fretwork is used to create an expansive, yet lightweight pattern for earrings.

STEEL

A number of different steels are used for jewelry-making purposes. Mild steel is easier to work with than tool steel, and is good for forging. Steel is challenging to solder because it oxidizes freely.

This classical steel brooch has a "molten" decorative surface which imitates the look of wax.

NICKEL

Nickel is both malleable and ductile. Harder than copper, gilding metal, and brass, it is particularly suitable for brooch pins and model-making. It can cause allergic reactions, and thus it is not often found in final jewelry forms.

PEWTER

A dark-gray, tin-based metal that is easily worked without annealing, pewter has far less strength than other metal alloys for jewelry. Some pewter alloys contain lead, which is a contaminant in a jewelry workshop.

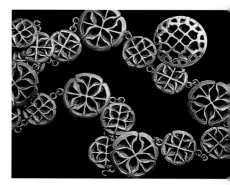

Carved fretwork forms are cast in pewter to form a decorative chain.

PLATINUM

A hard, heavy, inert metal, platinum is most often used for making settings, because it is stronger and more durable than gold and silver. It is a darker gray color than silver, and is about twice as heavy.

One ring in this series is set with a diamond held between two uprights, utilizing the strength of the platinum.

COPPER

A pinkish-red metal that is both malleable and ductile, copper is easily worked in a similar way to silver, although when pierced, it feels "sticky." Because of its high melting point, it is forgiving for soldering. It will turn black over time when exposed to air.

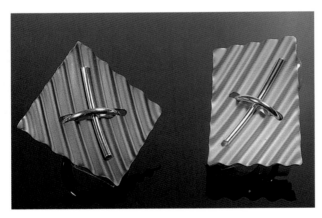

Fine copper wires are woven together to form a light, wispy neckpiece.

TITANIUM & ALUMINUM

Titanium is a hard, lightweight, gray-colored metal, while aluminum is similarly weighted and colored, but softer. Both metals can be anodized to produce a spectrum of bright colors.

Corrugated aluminum sheet captures a silver detail in these brightly colored anodized rings.

GILDING METAL

An alloy of copper, gilding metal is a golden-colored, malleable substance. If left exposed to the air for some time, it turns the color of copper. The substance bends, cuts, and generally reacts in a similar way to silver.

Gilding metal is pressed into gentle relief forms in these drop earrings.

Photoetching has been used to trace a shield shape with curling arms in this brass pin.

BRASS

An alloy of copper and zinc, brass is harder than copper. It is vulnerable when soldered using silver solder. If overheated, brass is inclined to melt due to its relatively low melting point.

PLASTICS

One of the most popular plastics for jewelry, Perspex sheet comes in many colors, and is easily cut, carved, and bent. Nylon is a tough, flexible material that can be colored using fabric dyes. Two-part epoxy or polyester resin is used for embedding and casting.

Quirky rings are made from silver, with plastic toothbrush heads forming two-toned detail.

ORGANIC MATERIALS

Wood, horn, and bone are often seen in jewelry forms, both as detailing and as the primary material. Most such materials can be carved and formed. Although generally easy to lathe-turn, the presence of grain can present problems.

Wood is carved and hollowed out to form a locket pendant with a silver catch.

STONES

Stones have been included in jewelry forms for centuries because of their value. A stone's value was traditionally measured by its rarity, color, and hardness. In some cultures, stones were also valued for their perceived magical and prophylactic properties. In modern terms, a gemstone is valued according to its weight, size, degree of perfection, brilliance, luster, transparency, availability, durability, and portability. Synthetic stones that mimic the qualities of gemstones can now be made, and can generally be purchased at a fraction of the price of the gemstone imitated.

FACETED

This term derives from the French word *facets*, meaning "little faces." In general, transparent stones are faceted to accentuate brilliance, heighten color, and to catch and reflect light, although some opaque stones are also faceted. Faceted stones conform to a number of standard cuts and shapes, but new ones are constantly being devised.

A large faceted heart-shaped Rubelite is the centerpiece for a romantic pendant.

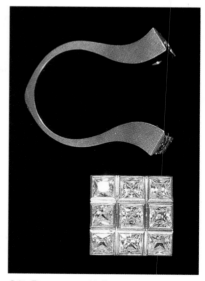

A faceted rectangular diamond complements the clean lines of a simple, modern ring.

ORGANIC

These "stones" are technically not considered stones in the true sense of the word, because they are neither mineral nor crystal. They are either a by-product of a living organism, or *were* once a living organism themselves. Examples frequently seen in a jewelry context are pearl, amber, coral, jet, tortoiseshell, and fossil.

A Mabe pearl illuminates a granulated gold brooch of radiating form.

Rough aquamarines are used as beads for a simple necklace, and as drops for earrings in this suite.

The rich red hues of coral are seen in this necklace, strung together with a gold and diamond clasp.

ALTERNATIVE STONES

Stones made from synthetics are often used as replacements for "real" stones; Cubic Zircons are frequently used in place of diamonds, for example. There are many synthetic materials available that imitate precious and semiprecious stones, as well as pearls. Other materials frequently seen in a jewelry context include glass, ceramic, stone, and pebbles.

Cubic Zircons create a blanket of light on the surface of this two-part ring.

CABOCHON

From the French word *cabouche*, meaning "head," the cabochon stone has a smoothly polished form which can be oval, round, tear-drop, or curved in some other shape. The cabochon cut is used for semiprecious stones, and for precious stones of a quality not sufficient to be cut as a faceted stone.

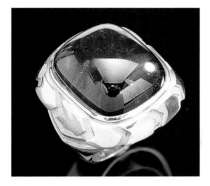

A large cabochon tourmaline is bezel-set and framed in a sumptuous carved gold ring.

SEMIPRECIOUS

Non-precious stones that are perceived as attractive enough when cut or polished to be used in a jewelry context are termed semiprecious. They tend to be found in larger quantities than precious stones. In the context of jewelry, these stones must be hard enough to ensure durability.

MOHS SCALE

This scale is named after the German mineralogist Friedrich Mohs, who devised it as an indicator of the approximate relative hardness of stones. The values in the Mohs scale are based on the stones' resistance to abrasion; the hardest—diamond—is rated 10, and the softest—talc—is rated 0.

DURABILITY

A stone is only suitable for jewelry if it is hard enough to endure daily wear and tear. The Mohs scale is a good indicator of this, as well as of which stones are likely to become damaged during jewelry fabrication. Emeralds are the softest of the precious stones, rating 7-7.5 on the Mohs scale.

MAINTENANCE

Settings and stones tend to collect grease and dirt. To soften and loosen such impurities, soak the piece in soapy, hot water, and use a soft brush to scrub the setting and stone from front to back. Organic stones need careful treatment, and pearls should not be soaked. Avoid thermal shock for all stones.

Labradorite is used as a complement to silver in this large pendant.

PRECIOUS

Diamonds, sapphires, rubies, and emeralds are considered to be precious because they are generally the most costly. The cleaner a precious stone is, the greater its value. Semiprecious stones of particularly good color and purity may, however, exceed the value of inferior precious stones.

Brightly colored semiprecious stones are used to enliven a decorative pendant form.

A square sapphire is flanked by two pear-shaped diamonds in a simple platinum ring.

SETTINGS

The setting can be described as the means by which a stone is secured into a piece of jewelry. Conventional jewelry tends to include the traditional claw setting, while contemporary jewelry is more inclined towards the clean lines of the tension, gypsy, and bezel settings. Settings such as the illusion or pavé setting are designed to create a visual impact. Pearls need not be set with metal, and are often held on a post and cup using a two-part epoxy resin.

CLAW

Claw settings are made of a crown of prongs, like slender metal fingers, attached to a bezel. Each prong ends in a bent-over end called a claw, which is pushed over the stone and above the girdle to hold it in place.

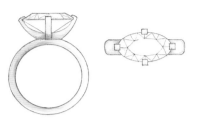

Fleur de lys and more traditional claws are combined to set a single diamond in this medieval-style ring.

GYPSY

A gypsy setting uses a thin flange that is created from the metal to form a bezel, into which the stone can then be set. The stone is sunk into the metal so that when set, it appears to be flush with the form of the piece.

A silver two-tiered ring is gypsy-set with diamonds on the shank and floating elevation.

BEZEL

A bezel setting surrounds the stone with a continuous fine wall of metal that stands higher than the girdle. This is then closed by pushing the wall down onto the stone to hold it in place.

A cluster of cabochon stones frame an intaglio centerpiece in this whimsical bezel-set pendant.

ILLUSION

An illusion setting is used to enhance the appearance of a small stone, making it seem larger than it is. The stone is set into a metal collet that creates a collar around it, with facets cut into it to catch and reflect light.

In these earrings, the appearance of the center stones is visually enhanced by the illusion setting.

PAVÉ

The term *pavé* derives from the French word for "paved." Small stones of a similar size, usually round, are grain-set close together to cover an area so that the amount of metal visible is minimal. The result is an area "paved" with stones.

This indulgent necklace is heavily pavéd with diamonds for an opulent look.

CHANNEL

Channel-set stones can appear as a line of stones set girdle to girdle, so that no metal appears between the stones. The stones are supported and set on two sides by two upright parallel walls, tracks, or channels.

Pink sapphires and diamonds are scattered around this ring using the natural gutters for channel setting.

TENSION

Tension settings rely on the strength of the metal to support and hold a stone in place via the use of tension. A stone will look as if it is captured on two sides between two pieces of metal, offering an open view of the stone.

Uncut emeralds and diamonds are captured by tension setting in these gold and steel rings.

GRAIN

For a grain setting, a number of grains are raised around a stone with a graver. This raises spur-like projections that are pushed over the girdle to hold the stone in. The grain is then rounded off with a graining tool.

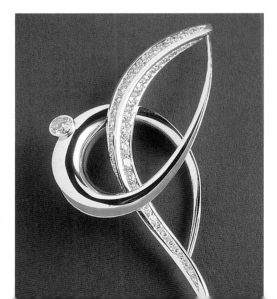

Graded diamonds are grain-set to flow with the line of an anticlastic brooch.

LINKS & JOINTS

Many jewelry forms require a certain level of flexibility, typically supplied by a link or joint between two or more parts. When choosing links and joints, it is necessary to take into account the degree and type of flexibility that is required for the piece. Linking can take many forms, from the most simple jump ring passed through a hole in each of the two units it joins—a flexible link—to the more sophisticated hinge joint, where movement is restricted to one plane. A highly flexible "blanket" of linked forms can be achieved by combining a number of links and joints, although this may take some planning. Because the range of links and joints is so diverse as to preclude showing all of them here, we have chosen a selection, illustrated in both drawings and photographs, to indicate some possible solutions.

Hinges are used to join the sections of this silver and velvet bracelet.

U-WIRE

This simple system restricts movement to horizontal flexibility, and is suitable for joining stone settings of various shapes.

HINGE

While a strong means of joining, this system restricts movement to one plane only. It is useful in bracelets, bangles, or pendants, but is not as well suited to necklaces.

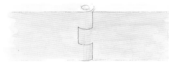

RIVET

A mechanical means of joining two parts that avoids the need for soldering, this system can be restrictive, unless some spacing is incorporated into the joint.

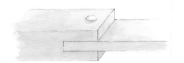

Aluminum bangles are articulated with a number of riveted joints which join the repeated units.

Large forged loops are interwoven and then locked with a jumping ring in this forged chain.

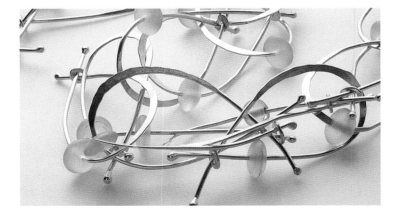

LINE

Movement is restricted so that collets or forms appear in a line. The linking rods need to be strong, and the slots must be tightly fitted.

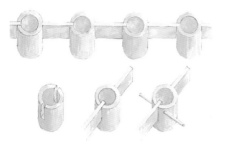

RING & BAR

This system allows moderate vertical flexibility, and allows for horizontal flexibility to be varied. It need not be soldered, so long as the link wires are robust.

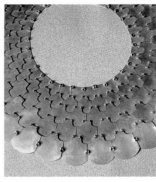

Rivets are used to fasten the many tendril-like arms of this silver necklace.

BALL & BAR

In this method of linking, a ball is encircled by a ring, and together they hold the bar in place. This system allows for a great deal of universal movement,

BALL & SOCKET

Using the principle of the universal joint, this system allows for a great deal of flexibility in all directions.

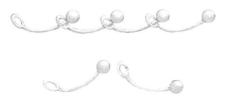

An armour-like collar is articulated by the repetition of a simple linking system.

DOUBLE ARM SLIDE

Highly flexible and similar in principle to the ball and bar, this system allows two forms to move together, or in line.

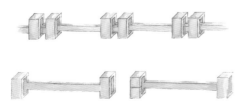

Loops with beaded ends are passed through the center of forged discs to articulate this necklace.

FITTINGS

Fittings are hand-made attachments that allow jewelry to be worn. Because they are primarily involved with function, they must be strong and durable—a broken fitting may well render the piece unwearable. Whenever possible, a fitting should be fabricated as an integral part of the piece, rather than as an additional element, so that it complements the form for which it is required. Fittings such as earring hooks or "S" catches are made easily by hand, while others, such as box catches or swivel cufflink fittings, require a reasonable level of skill.

EARRINGS

Earring fittings come in many different varieties, and are available for both pierced and non-pierced ears. Pierced fittings include posts (both threaded and non-threaded), hooks, and hoops. Butterfly or scroll backs are generally used to secure posts, although screw fittings can also be used. Fittings for non-pierced ears include clips, both plain and of the omega style, and screw fittings. An omega-style clip can also be used as a back for a pierced fitting.

Integral threaded posts bridge a central space in these silver earrings.

A post coupled with an omega clip is used to secure these diamond earrings.

Post & scroll

Clip

Clip hook

Threaded post & scroll

Omega clip

Screw fitting

BROOCHES

A fixed brooch back is characterized by its fixed length, and is used because of the solidity of its back, which gives it strength. Separate fitting components, such as those that comprise the pin, safety-catch and fichu back, and the pull-out catch back, allow the back components to be assembled at different distances, but these are not as sturdy as the fixed back. Brooch pins are usually fitted with the joint on the right and the catch facing downward on the left; the weight of the brooch is used to help keep the pin from escaping the catch.

Simple double pins add to the individuality of these brooches.

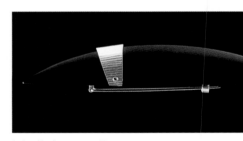

A claw-like form captured by a silver collar is secured as a brooch with a single pin.

Fixed brooch back

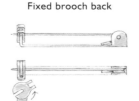

Pin, safety-catch & fichu

Pull-out catch

CATCHES

Catches are generally made so that a section of a chain, bracelet, or neckpiece can be secured after passing around the relevant part of the body. Although the bolt ring is the most commonly found type of catch, swivel and lobster claw catches are generally more secure. Perhaps the simplest style of catch, the oriental-style "S" catch can eventually harden with continued use, and may thus need re-annealing in time.

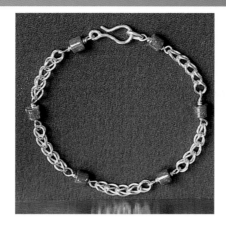

Bolt ring

Lobster claw

Swivel

A simple hook is used as a catch to secure this stone-set chain bracelet.

The bar of this toggle catch becomes a feature as the ends are set in diamonds.

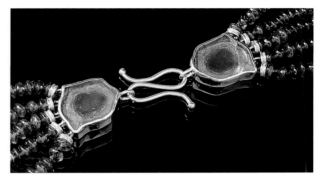

An extended "S" catch is used to secure an adventurine bead necklace that ends in tourmaline filials.

CUFFLINKS

Function defines the form of the swivel link fitting; as such, it is generally constructed in a standard way and in a standard form. Toggle and chain links are more variable in their construction, as their backs and fronts take a number of different shapes and forms. Any soldered joints must be strong enough to endure the pressure of the wearer leaning on the joint by accident.

Gold stone-set cufflinks are finished with easy-to-wear swivel link backs.

Chain link   Swivel link   Hinged toggle

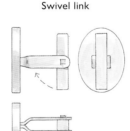

Highly polished cufflinks with fancy bar backs are linked by chains.

The finish and texture of a piece of jewelry are often overlooked, both in the process of fabrication and as a design consideration. Finishing and texturing can be very time-consuming, and often require careful planning in order to avoid damage to textures, and to ensure the fluidity of the assembly process. In general, a piece can be cleaned and a finish applied before assembly; indeed, this may be necessary, as once assembled, it can be hard to reach all areas. Conventional jewelry tends to be highly polished, but there are many textures to choose from. Some textural effects, such as mokumé gane, are sophisticated enough to act as the central feature in the piece.

Sweeping lines are satin-finished in this striking ring.

POLISHING

The first stage of polishing is the removal of file marks and any other surface blemishes using an abrasive. The surface is then polished further by rubbing with successively finer abrasives. A brilliant shine can be achieved either by hand or by machine, but both methods are time-consuming.

OXIDIZING

Because certain metals will oxidize naturally over time when exposed to air and dampness, older pieces of jewelry tend to be oxidized. Oxidizing can also be achieved by a chemical process that blackens the surface of the metal; this can then be worked back mechanically for a more natural, aged effect.

MILL-PRESSING

This is a simple method of imparting a pattern onto metal. Paper, or other materials such as fabric or wool, are rolled through a rolling mill with an annealed sheet of metal. The sheet of metal and pattern will elongate as it is rolled. This process will not work with metals that are harder than the rollers of the mill.

Silver earrings are oxidized, creating warm deep brown and black tones.

A collection of brooches are mill-pressed to give them their subtle surfaces.

ETCHING

Etching is a process that uses acid to corrode metal. An etch-resist solution is used to protect parts of the metal, while the exposed areas are eaten away. Etching is used to create recesses for enameling as well as surface texture. Different metals require different acids and different etch-resist solutions.

PATINATION

Patination is the process by which metals are colored by exposure to a variety of chemicals. Copper, bronze, gilding metal, brass, and silver are all suitable, as are some plate surfaces. Metal that is to be patinated must be completely clean.

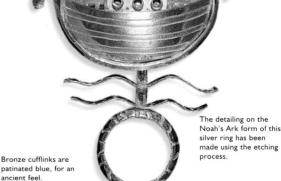

The detailing on the Noah's Ark form of this silver ring has been made using the etching process.

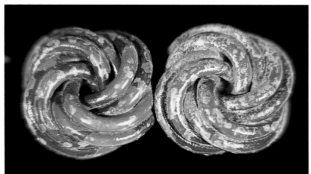

Bronze cufflinks are patinated blue, for an ancient feel.

GRANULATION

Granulation is derived from the Latin word *granulum*, the diminutive of "grain." In this process, small grains of metal are joined to a surface, traditionally by fusion. This method works best with gold, but silver can also be used. The fixing of grains can also be achieved by the careful use of solder.

Gold earrings are given a delicate pattern using wire work and granulation.

ENGRAVING

This is the process of removing surface metal to create a design using a sharp steel tool called a graver. Engraving can be used for surface decoration, lettering, and for cutting back for champlevé in enamelling. Cameos and intaglios are made by engraving gemstones.

A sculptural ring is engraved all over in an intricate pattern.

INLAY

In this process, one metal is fused or soldered into another metal in a recess cut by engraving, chasing, milling, drilling, or piercing. The surface is then filed flush so that the recesses become clearly defined. This method can be applied to sheet or cast forms to create lines or areas of contrasting color.

These earrings are adorned by two tapering columns of inlaid red and yellow gold.

LEAF & FOIL

Covering a surface with silver or gold can be achieved by the application of thin sheets of metal known as "leaf." The effect created is a soft sheen rather than a polished finish. Imitation gold and silver leaf is also available, and is less expensive than the real thing. Foil is slightly heavier than leaf, and is typically used for enamelling.

These two pairs of open silver earrings have been finished with gold leaf.

RETICULATION

Originally called *samorodok*, Russian for "born of itself," reticulation comes from the Latin word *reticulum*, the diminutive of "net." The process creates a web- or net-like effect by the application of heat to metal to a stage beyond annealing, but before melting.

This locket pendant in silver is made from reticulated sheet.

PLATING

"Plate" is a fine covering of metal that is deposited on a metal surface by electrolytic plating. Plate will not blur detail, nor will it mask any blemishes, and so the final finish must be achieved before plating. An object need not be plated in its entirety; areas can be masked out. Plate does not resist abrasion well.

A silver frog sits on a twig made of gold-plated silver.

MOKUMÉ GANE

In Japanese, *mokumé* means "wood grain," and *gane* means "metal." In this process, layers of metal are fused together to form a mokumé laminate. A pattern is then made by cutting into the surface, filing back, and rolling flush the layers of metal exposed by filing.

Titanium, copper, and silver are used to make this subtly-patterned mokumé gane brooch.

ENAMELLING

Enamel is a form of glass, and enamelling is the process whereby this glass is fused to metal by heating to create areas of color. The color of enamel can range from primaries to pastels; it can be opaque, translucent, or transparent, and can have a gloss or matte finish. Despite its relative fragility, enamelling is an exciting art; the different techniques, colors, levels of opacity, and finishes possible with this process can produce unique effects that will enhance jewelry forms significantly. It is a time-consuming and labor-intensive technique, however, and requires patience and skill.

CHAMPLEVÉ

Named for the French word for "raised field," in this process recesses are made in a sheet of metal by engraving, etching, photoetching, or stamping, and then filled with enamel. The base of the recess can be textured. The sheet of enamel created is level, with intersecting areas of metal defining the recessed areas, creating a pattern.

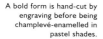

A bold form is hand-cut by engraving before being champlevé-enamelled in pastel shades.

A pair of round pendants are champlevé-enamelled on photoetched silver.

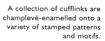

A collection of cufflinks are champlevé-enamelled onto a variety of stamped patterns and motifs.

The detail is hand-cut for champlevé in two brooches depicting colorful jay feathers.

24

BASSE-TAILLE

From the French term *basse-taille*, meaning "low-cut," in this process the surface of the metal to be enamelled is decorated with a low relief design, creating a surface decoration that can be seen through translucent and transparent enamels. The surface texture reflects light, and the depth of the cutting will influence the depth of the color of the enamel.

In this brooch, enamel applied in the basse-taille method accentuates the gradations of color across the piece.

CLOISONNÉ

From the French word *cloison*, meaning "cell," in this technique, small cells of enamel are enclosed by thin walls of metal wire called cloisonné wire. This fine, flat wire is first fashioned into a shape, and then attached to the surface either in a layer of flux, or by soldering. The areas defined by the cloisonné wires are then filled with enamel.

This shield-shaped brooch shows silver enamelled with patterns made by the cloisonné technique.

PLIQUE-À-JOUR

From the French term *plique-à-jour*, meaning "braid letting in daylight," this enamel has no backing, so that it can be viewed from both sides. Cells are cut out of a metal sheet and then filled, to achieve windows of enamel that are held to the walls of the cells by capillary action. This form of enamelling is very vulnerable—any flexing of the sheet will cause the enamel to fracture.

These two hollow pendants are colored with plique-à-jour enamelling.

PAINTING

Also known as Limoges enamelling, in this method fine enamel paint is applied to a base of enamel to create an image. Often used on an opaque white enamel base, the pastel quality of enamel painting makes it particularly well suited for portraiture. The design can be painted directly onto the white base, or the outline can be traced and then transferred.

In this painted enamel brooch, a view of a sumptuous country house is depicted.

The range of shapes and forms in which a piece of jewelry can be made is virtually infinite. The following pages are illustrated with a rich variety of drawings and photographic images, designed to represent a broad spectrum of choice within the many different categories and styles of

Directory of Shape & Form

jewelry. Examples range from classic designs and materials to more contemporary ones, and from simpler pieces to those that are made using unusual and innovative materials and techniques.

The shape and form of earrings on the ear are restricted in terms of size because of their proportion in relation to the size of the ear. Pierced earrings should not be too heavy, otherwise they will drag the ear down, causing the lobe to be distorted, or the earring to tilt away from the ear. Posts are particularly vulnerable, and may need to be repaired in their lifetime. A close-fit jump ring around the soldered end of the post creates a greater surface area for the joint,

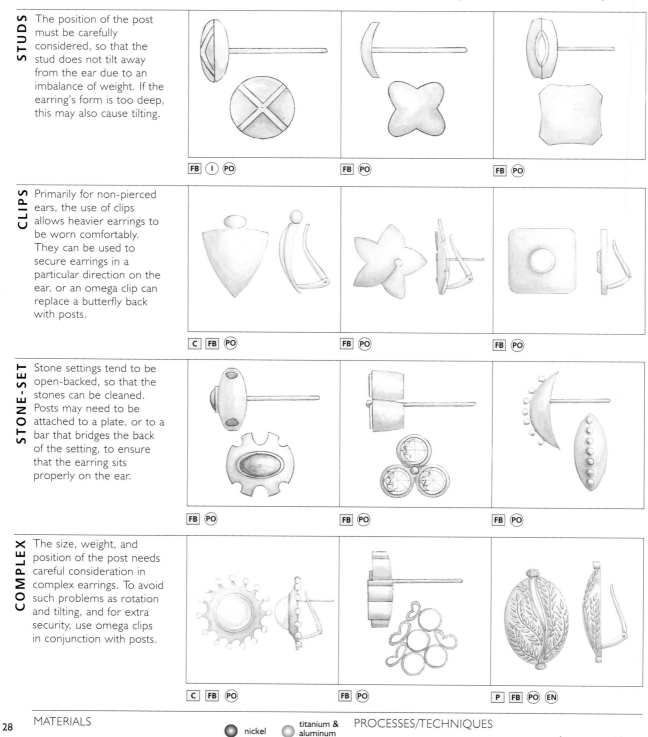

STUDS The position of the post must be carefully considered, so that the stud does not tilt away from the ear due to an imbalance of weight. If the earring's form is too deep, this may also cause tilting.

FB (I) (PO) · FB (PO) · FB (PO)

CLIPS Primarily for non-pierced ears, the use of clips allows heavier earrings to be worn comfortably. They can be used to secure earrings in a particular direction on the ear, or an omega clip can replace a butterfly back with posts.

C FB (PO) · FB (PO) · FB (PO)

STONE-SET Stone settings tend to be open-backed, so that the stones can be cleaned. Posts may need to be attached to a plate, or to a bar that bridges the back of the setting, to ensure that the earring sits properly on the ear.

FB (PO) · FB (PO) · FB (PO)

COMPLEX The size, weight, and position of the post needs careful consideration in complex earrings. To avoid such problems as rotation and tilting, and for extra security, use omega clips in conjunction with posts.

C FB (PO) · FB (PO) · P FB (PO) (EN)

MATERIALS

PROCESSES/TECHNIQUES

- gold
- silver
- platinum
- copper
- brass
- gilding metal
- nickel
- pewter
- steel
- titanium & aluminum
- organic
- plastic

FB fabrication
FW fretwork
F forging
P pressing
RC repoussé & chasing
C casting
ST special techniques
E enamelling

adding strength and durability. Allergic reactions to metal—especially nickel—is a common problem, so posts should always be made from either silver, gold, or platinum. In individual cases, the size of an earlobe and the position of the pierced hole may result in a need to alter the position of the post, and a larger butterfly back or an omega clip may be required to help hold the earring in position.

STUDS

○ FB PO

○ ○ FB PO O

○ P FB MP

○ ○ P FB O PO

CLIPS

○ ○ FB I PO O

○ C FB PO

○ ○ P FB PO

STONE-SET

○ P FB PO

○ ○ FB G PO

○ P FB PO

○ SP FB EN PO

COMPLEX

○ C FB PO

○ ○ F FB PO

○ ○ FB ET PO

FINISHES

PO polish
MP mill pressing
ET etching
EN engraving
R reticulation
L leaf or foil
PL plating
O oxidizing
PA patination
G granulation
M mokumé gane
I inlay

STONES

P precious
SP semiprecious
O organic
S synthetic & other

29

Historically, hooks and hoops were early examples of pierced earrings. They were generally simple to make and easy to wear, and did not rely on the scroll back. Contemporary pieces are perhaps more inventive and technically sophisticated, but the forms remain equally as satisfying. The hoop earring may be a simple sleeper with a pendant form, or a pierced fitting with a scroll back. Larger forms may need to be hollowed out to avoid excessive weight, as

SIMPLE HOOKS

Consider the length of the hooks. If they are too short, the earrings can be accidentally pushed out of the lobe. Solid hook-to-drop earrings can be vulnerable in that the hook is more likely to break off.

FB PO FB PO FB PO

FANCY HOOKS

Slight variations made to a simple hook can add a great deal of character to the whole piece. Additional interest can be added to the shape and form of a hook by employing a number of techniques, including casting, forging, twisting, or bending.

C FB PO FB PO FB PO

SIMPLE HOOPS

The act of opening and closing hoops can cause wear and pose difficulty. Instructions regarding their use and care should be included if possible, to reduce the risk of breakage, and to avoid unnecessary repairs.

FB PO C FB PO F FB PO

FANCY HOOPS

Significant weight may be added to hoops through casting, and by the addition of simple elements to their form. If making fancy hoops, consider the overall weight of the earring, to avoid any pulling on the earlobe.

FB PO P FB PO P FB PO

MATERIALS

- gold
- silver
- platinum
- copper
- brass
- gilding metal
- nickel
- pewter
- steel
- titanium & aluminum
- organic
- plastic

PROCESSES/TECHNIQUES

| FB | fabrication | F | forging | RC | repoussé & chasing | ST | special techniques |
| FW | fretwork | P | pressing | C | casting | E | enamelling |

hoops that are too heavy tend not to sit well, and can pull on the ear. As with pierced posts, $\frac{1}{32}$ in (0.8mm) diameter wire is most suitable for the section that passes through the ear. This wire need not always be fabricated in a round shape—a minimal amount of simple forging can be used to give an ear wire a different shape, and to strengthen it. The use of hardened wire will help prevent distortion in hooks and hoops.

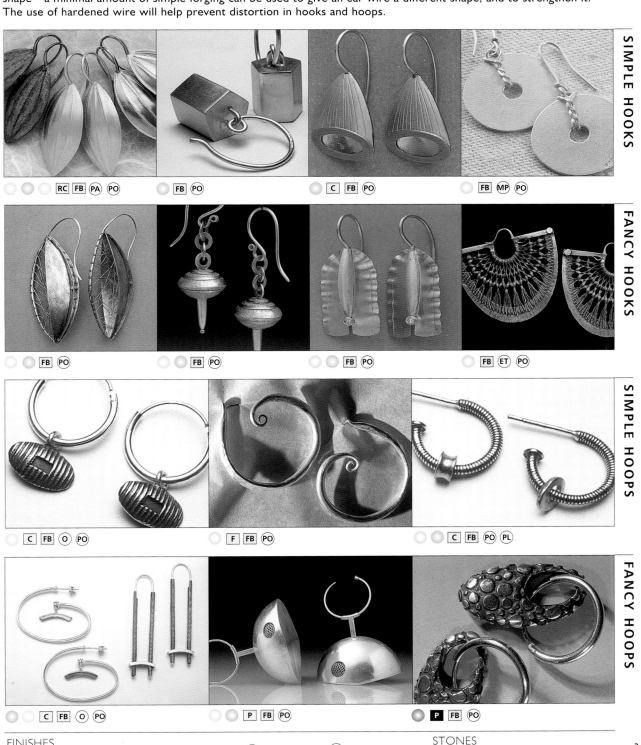

SIMPLE HOOKS

○ ○ ○ ○ ☐RC☐ ☐FB☐ ⓅA ⓅO   ○ ☐FB☐ ⓅO   ○ ☐C☐ ☐FB☐ ⓅO   ○ ☐FB☐ ⓂP ⓅO

FANCY HOOKS

○ ○ ☐FB☐ ⓅO   ○ ○ ☐FB☐ ⓅO   ○ ○ ☐FB☐ ⓅO   ○ ☐FB☐ ⒺT ⓅO

SIMPLE HOOPS

○ ☐C☐ ☐FB☐ Ⓞ ⓅO   ○ ☐F☐ ☐FB☐ ⓅO   ○ ○ ☐C☐ ☐FB☐ ⓅO ⓅL

FANCY HOOPS

○ ○ ○ ☐C☐ ☐FB☐ Ⓞ ⓅO   ○ ○ ☐P☐ ☐FB☐ ⓅO   ○ ● ☐P☐ ☐FB☐ ⓅO

FINISHES

ⓅO polish   ⒺT etching   Ⓡ reticulation
ⓂP mill pressing   ⒺN engraving   Ⓛ leaf or foil

ⓅL plating   Ⓖ granulation
Ⓞ oxidizing   Ⓜ mokumé gane
ⓅA patination   Ⓘ inlay

STONES

☐P☐ precious   ☐O☐ organic
☐SP☐ semiprecious   ☐S☐ synthetic & other

31

EARRINGS • MISCELLANEOUS

Earrings and rings are probably the most popular form of jewelry sold today, and many styles are available as a result. While earrings are relatively smaller in form than other types of jewelry, to some they are the lipstick of jewelry; without them, one can feel naked. Simple forms tend to be the most enduring style of earring, often defying fashion, and suitable for the context of everyday life. Fancy earrings, on the other hand, can evoke glamour and a sense of

SIMPLE

Simple by nature, this category is both easy and comfortable to wear, and is thus most likely to be worn on a daily basis. Ensure that there are no details that can catch loose threads or hair, such as loose claws or tight gaps.

P   FB   PO

FB   PO

FB   G   PO

MIXED-MEDIA

Some modern materials are lighter and brighter than more traditional materials, and thus work particularly well in earrings. Such earrings will nonetheless require silver, gold, or platinum posts, to avoid an allergic reaction in the wearer.

P   FB   PO

FB   PO

FB   PO

STONE-SET

The length, color, and movement often seen in stone-set earrings lend a feeling of sophistication. The backs of the stones should be accessible, as they can collect dirt and may require cleaning.

FB   PO

FB   PO

FB   PO

FANCY

For earrings that dangle, the senses should be considered; the sound of jangling materials can be unexpected and unwelcome—or it can add an element of fun. Also consider texture, for both dangling and sedentary earrings, to add additional interest.

FB   PP   PO

FB   PO

C   FB   PO

MATERIALS

- gold
- silver
- platinum
- copper
- brass
- gilding metal
- nickel
- pewter
- steel
- titanium & aluminum
- organic
- plastic

PROCESSES/TECHNIQUES

| FB | fabrication | F | forging | RC | repoussé & chasing | ST | special techniques |
| FW | fretwork | P | pressing | C | casting | E | enamelling |

style. They can be useful as a finishing touch for a simple outfit, to make it look expensive or sophisticated, or simply to add color and fun. Whether simple, glamorous, or fine, a single earring should weigh no more than ⅓ oz (10g), to ensure comfort. Because of their proximity to hair and clothing, earrings can cause irritation. Elements that can catch loose threads and hair, or scratch the neck if swung, should be avoided.

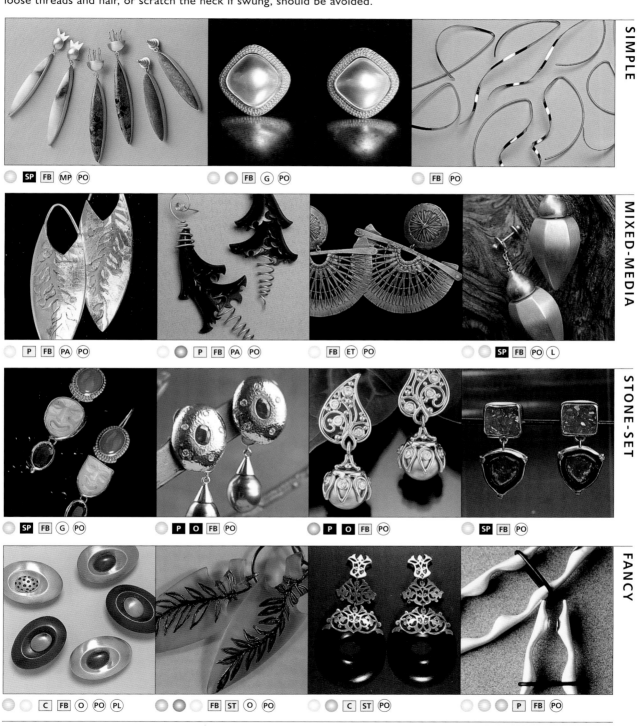

SIMPLE

○ SP FB MP PO   ○ ○ FB G PO   ○ FB PO

MIXED-MEDIA

○ P FB PA PO   ○ ● P FB PA PO   ○ FB ET PO   ○ ○ ● SP FB PO L

STONE-SET

○ SP FB G PO   ○ P O FB PO   ○ P O FB PO   ○ SP FB PO

FANCY

○ ○ C FB O PO PL   ○ ○ ○ FB ST O PO   ○ ○ C ST PO   ○ ○ ○ ○ P FB PO

33

NECKLACES

Necklaces can take many forms, either as repeated units, or as a collection of elements that culminate in a focal point. Care must be taken to ensure that the links provide sufficient flexibility, and do not bunch together when worn. The catch on a necklace is often the weakest link; while commonly used, commercial bolt rings should be avoided if possible, because they rely on a tiny spring that can easily be broken. An integral catch is the best way to finish off a

SIMPLE

Simple need not mean dull so long as sufficient attention is paid to detail. Subtle details such as relief can add to the three-dimensional quality of a form without appearing overstated. The finish of a piece can also draw attention to the detail contained therein.

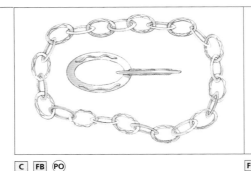

C FB PO

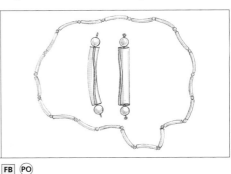

FB PO

SHORT

Particularly suited to daily wear, short necklaces are generally comfortable and easily worn—although they can also be glamorous. The average length for a short necklace is 16 in (400mm), but this length can be varied according to preference.

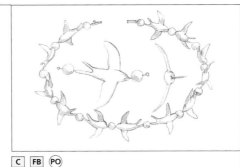

C FB PO

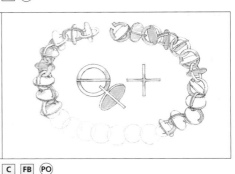

C FB PO

LONG

Long necklaces can easily be passed over the head, so they generally do not need to have a catch. Length can also create versatility; doubling-up a piece will create a different look and effect than when it is worn as a single strand, and a catch may then be necessary.

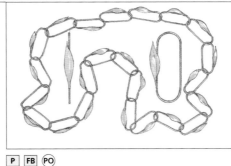

P FB PO

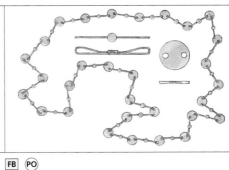

FB PO

FANCY

Fancy need not mean complex, but intricate forms, details, and textures can all add interest to a piece. If a necklace has a great deal of movement, stone settings or enamel work may be vulnerable.

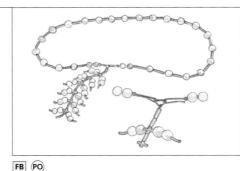

FB PO

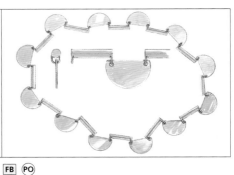

FB PO

34

MATERIALS

- gold
- silver
- platinum
- copper
- brass
- gilding metal
- nickel
- pewter
- steel
- titanium & aluminum
- organic
- plastic

PROCESSES/TECHNIQUES

| FB | fabrication | F | forging | RC | repoussé & chasing | ST | special techniques |
| FW | fretwork | P | pressing | C | casting | E | enamelling |

piece, and may even be used as the feature or centerpiece of the necklace. Expensive necklaces may require the security of an additional safety fitting such as a chain or an extra catch, so that if the main catch fails the piece is less likely to be lost. Such simple fittings as closed "S" catches, often seen in traditional oriental jewelry, are easily made and durable. When designing a necklace, avoid adding details that may snag clothing or catch on fabric or hair.

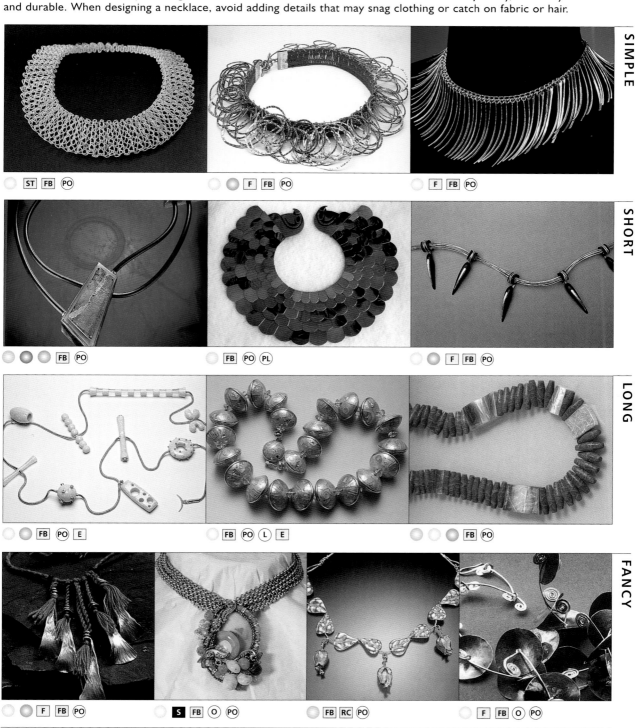

SIMPLE

ST FB PO   F FB PO   F FB PO

SHORT

FB PO   FB PO PL   F FB PO

LONG

FB PO E   FB PO L E   FB PO

FANCY

F FB PO   S FB O PO   FB RC PO   F FB O PO

FINISHES

PO polish
MP mill pressing
ET etching
EN engraving
R reticulation
L leaf or foil
PL plating
O oxidizing
PA patination
G granulation
M mokumé gane
I inlay

STONES

P precious
SP semiprecious
O organic
S synthetic & other

35

NECKPIECES

Neckpieces differ from necklaces in that they tend to emphasize one or more focal points. Alternatively, the emphasis may be upon the way in which the neckpiece is worn, as is the case with a choker. In such close-fitting or solid forms as the choker, the size and shape must be carefully considered, and sizing trials on the person's neck may be necessary during manufacture. The neck can be a difficult body part to work with; a neckpiece generally has to be able to flex

SIMPLE

The fabrication of simple neckpiece forms can be difficult, requiring great skill and judgment. Simplicity in a neckpiece doesn't always mean comfort, however; heavy, solid forms can be uncomfortable if they cause pressure points on the neck or shoulder.

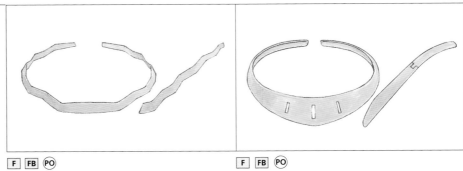

F | FB | PO   F | FB | PO

BEADED

If beads are strung on thread, the piece may be vulnerable; wire may be used as an alternative to thread. Knotting between the beads will reduce loss in the case of breakage, as well as extending the length of the piece; it will also reduce the overall bead content.

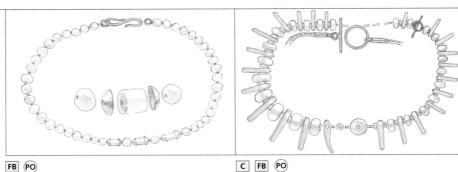

FB | PO   C | FB | PO

CHOKER

Stiff, upright chokers may cause discomfort; sharp ends should always be avoided. Flexible sizing is advisable with this format, unless the piece is being specially fabricated for a specific individual.

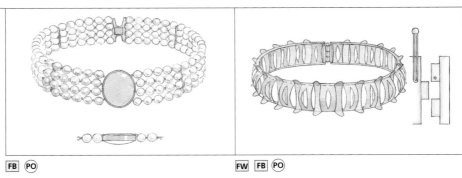

FB | PO   FW | FB | PO

FANCY

Fancy neckpieces can be complex in either design or technique—or both. They can be made to contain a number of different joints, weights, links, and materials. They may also be created to be worn in more than one way or format.

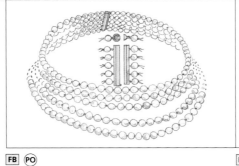

FB | PO   FB | PO

MATERIALS

- ● gold
- ○ silver
- ● platinum
- ● copper
- ● brass
- ○ gilding metal
- ● nickel
- ● pewter
- ● steel
- ○ titanium & aluminum
- ● organic
- ○ plastic

PROCESSES/TECHNIQUES

| FB | fabrication | F | forging | RC | repoussé & chasing | ST | special techniques |
| FW | fretwork | P | pressing | C | casting | E | enamelling |

around the neck as well as over the shoulders. Linked forms that are movable on one plane only are therefore unsuitable on their own, and must be used in combination with links that can move in other planes as well, so that the piece can flex in all necessary directions. A pearl neckpiece or necklace worn close to the skin daily will need biannual re-threading, as the threads will absorb the body's natural oils and may cause the pearls to discolor.

SIMPLE

○ ST FB PO   ○ F FB PO   ○ F FB PO

BEADED

○ SP O FB R PO   ○ SP FB L PO E   ○ ○ C FB PO PL

CHOKER

○ ○ ○ F FB PO   ○ ○ ○ ST FB R PO   ○ ○ P FB PO

FANCY

○ ○ ○ SP O FB I PO L   ○ F FB PO   ○ ○ ○ ○ FB ET PA PO

FINISHES

PO polish
MP mill pressing
ET etching
EN engraving
R reticulation
L leaf or foil
PL plating
O oxidizing
PA patination
G granulation
M mokumé gane
I inlay

STONES

P precious
SP semiprecious
O organic
S synthetic & other

37

PENDANTS

Generally speaking, there are fewer restrictions in the materials and forms that can be used for pendants than in other forms of jewelry. This is because the pendant does not generally suffer the wear and tear to which other pieces of jewelry are typically subject. Pendants do, however, often come into contact with skin, so materials that could cause allergic reactions should be avoided, as should scratchy details, or details that may catch in the fine fabric or threads of

ON THE CHAIN

This method of hanging a pendant incorporates the chain as part of the form of the piece, either permanently, or as a removable part. Hanging a pendant in this way is a useful means of avoiding the use of a bail or loop fitting.

FB PO EN   C FB PO   P FB PO L

FROM THE CHAIN

A pendant that hangs from a chain will require a bail or a loop fitting from which to hang. Avoid sharp edges on the fitting, as both it and the chain will wear. Careful positioning of the bail or loop may be necessary to balance the piece.

P FB PO   P FB PO   FB PO

CENTERPIECES

A pendant is often the focal point of a neckpiece. A complex, eye-catching visual effect may be achieved by considering in combination the form, size, color, texture, and detail of the piece.

FB PO EN   C FB PO   C FB PO

FANCY

The complexity and function of a fancy piece is often reliant on the accuracy of its fabrication. High levels of skill may be required to ensure that the detail contained in a piece is visually crisp, and that it functions as it should.

P FB PO   C FB PO   FB PO

38

MATERIALS

- ○ gold
- ○ silver
- ○ platinum
- ● copper
- ○ brass
- ○ gilding metal
- ● nickel
- ● pewter
- ● steel
- ○ titanium & aluminum
- ○ organic
- ○ plastic

PROCESSES/TECHNIQUES

| FB | fabrication | F | forging | RC | repoussé & chasing | ST | special techniques |
| FW | fretwork | P | pressing | C | casting | E | enamelling |

clothing. Some pendants are made to be detachable, so that they can be removed from their original chain and attached to a necklace with a special fitting, to dress up or enliven that piece. By virtue of its usual positioning as the centerpiece on a chain, a pendant can have a great impact, demanding attention with eye-catching detail or underlying symbolism. Other types of pendants, such as lockets, are functional as well as decorative.

Row 1:
○ ◉ FB MP PO   ○ ○ FB PO   ○ FB PO

Row 2:
○ ○ ◉ F FB I PO   ○ ○ P E FB PO   ○ ◉ P FB PO

Row 3:
○ ○ S P FB O PO   ○ ◉ SP RC FB PO   ○ ◉ FB PO PL   ◉ P O C FB PO

Row 4:
○ ○ ◉ P SP FB G PO   ○ P FB O PO   ○ ○ P FB PO E

FINISHES

PO polish	ET etching	R reticulation	PL plating
MP mill pressing	EN engraving	L leaf or foil	O oxidizing
			PA patination

G granulation
M mokumé gane
I inlay

STONES

P precious   O organic
SP semiprecious   S synthetic & other

39

BROOCHES & PINS

The visual impact of a brooch or a decorative pin is typically a simple, pleasing combination of form, color, and detail. The pin or post that is affixed to the back of a brooch, used to fasten it onto clothing, is unfortunately often seen as purely utilitarian, and thus paid no attention. This decision can cheapen the overall effect of the piece. In reality, the back of a brooch is an area of importance that can add interest and satisfaction to both maker and wearer. Because

SIMPLE

A small decorative pin is often preferable to a larger brooch because it can be easily worn on the lapel or on lightweight fabrics. Pins can be inherently simple, and can project a sense of completion.

FB PO

FB PO

C FB PO

SINGLE PINS

The single-pinned brooch should be fastened so that the pin points from right to left. The opening mechanism of the catch should point downward, allowing gravity to help keep the pin from coming undone.

FB PO

FB PO

FB PO

DOUBLE PINS

Double pins are better suited to large, heavy, or long pieces than single pins. The double pin allows the piece to be positioned securely, keeping excess movement to a minimum. Although relatively easy to make, this is a more sophisticated form of pin.

RC FB PO

FB I PO

FB PO EN

NARRATIVE

This type of brooch is the perfect medium for the pictorial expression of the wearer's personality. The frame can be ambiguous, used to simply contain the center, or it can form an integral part of the narrative.

FB I PO

C FB EN PO

FB PO EN

40

MATERIALS

- ○ gold
- ○ silver
- ○ platinum
- ● copper
- ○ brass
- ○ gilding metal
- ● nickel
- ● pewter
- ● steel
- ○ titanium & aluminum
- ○ organic
- ○ plastic

PROCESSES/TECHNIQUES

| FB | fabrication | F | forging | RC | repoussé & chasing | ST | special techniques |
| FW | fretwork | P | pressing | C | casting | E | enamelling |

the pin or post is often the most vulnerable part of a brooch, harder materials should be used, and the solder join between the fitting and body of the piece should have as large a contact surface as possible, to create strength in the joint, and for greater durability. The position of the pin on the back of the piece should also be considered, to ensure that it is balanced. Double pins are preferable for larger pieces, as they secure the brooch more firmly in position.

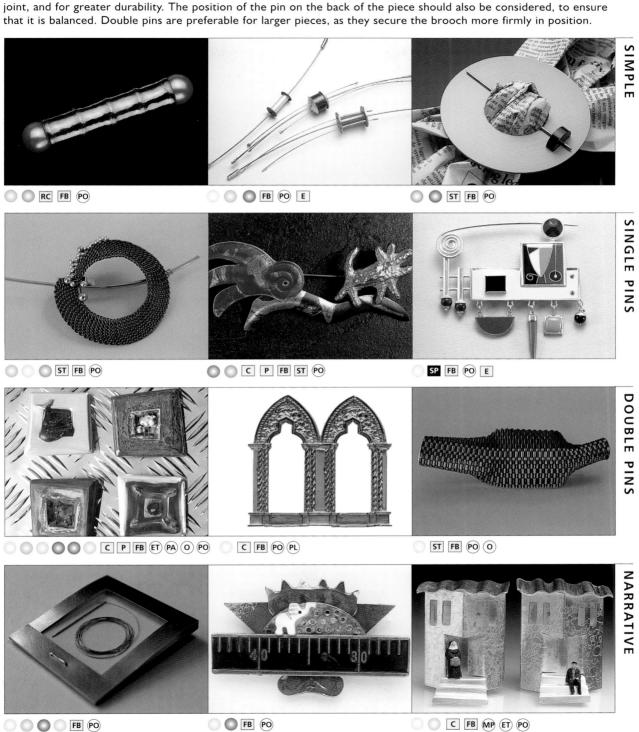

RC FB PO

FB PO E

ST FB PO

ST FB PO

C P FB ST PO

SP FB PO E

C P FB ET PA O PO

C FB PO PL

ST FB PO O

FB PO

FB PO

C FB MP ET PO

FINISHES

STONES

41

PO polishing
MP mill pressing
ET etching
EN engraving
R reticulation
L leaf or foil
PL plating
O oxidizing
PA patination
G granulation
M mokumé gane
I inlay

P precious
SP semiprecious
O organic
S synthetic & other

BROOCHES • UNUSUAL

In some instances, it is the fitting of a brooch that characterizes the piece as unusual. One such fitting is the Celtic type, distinguishable by its shape. The Celtic fitting generally requires a heavier fabric, because the pins used are often robust, and might damage finer fabrics. These fittings rely, to a degree, on weight for closure. Where the brooch has a functional element to it that can be opened and closed, such as that in a frame or a locket, consider the relative

CELTIC

The material from which a Celtic pin is made must be of a heavier gauge than that used for conventional pins. In many Celtic-style brooches, both the weight of the piece and a fixed position hold the fabric in place once it is passed over the pin.

ST FB PO   RC FB PO   C FB PO

MULTIMEDIA

Stones can be used to add highlights, color, and visual impact to a brooch form. The limited amount of wear on brooches means that delicate materials and processes can be used.

FB PO   RC FB PO   FB PO

FRAME

The fittings for frames may be fixed; however, the contents can be changed if the frame is made to be flexible. Consider whether the frame should be made to be watertight, to exclude—or perhaps contain—liquid.

FB EN PO   FB PO   FB PO

FANCY

An integral pin or fitting on a brooch will enhance the look of the piece significantly. For example, on a circular brooch, which may suit a curved rather than a straight pin, the clasp may be fabricated as part of the form.

FW FB PO   F FB PO   RC FB PO

MATERIALS

- gold
- silver
- platinum
- copper
- brass
- gilding metal
- nickel
- pewter
- steel
- titanium & aluminum
- organic
- plastic

PROCESSES/TECHNIQUES

| FB | fabrication | F | forging | RC | repoussé & chasing | ST | special techniques |
| FW | fretwork | P | pressing | C | casting | E | enamelling |

strength of the miniaturized mechanism, to avoid breakage. Delicate stones and settings are well suited to brooches, as little wear and tear occurs when a brooch is worn. Because fabric lies between the wearer's skin and the brooch, there is little likelihood of discoloration to some materials, such as silver. Flat backs on a brooch can look rather crude, so gentle rounding should be considered, to add interest to the piece.

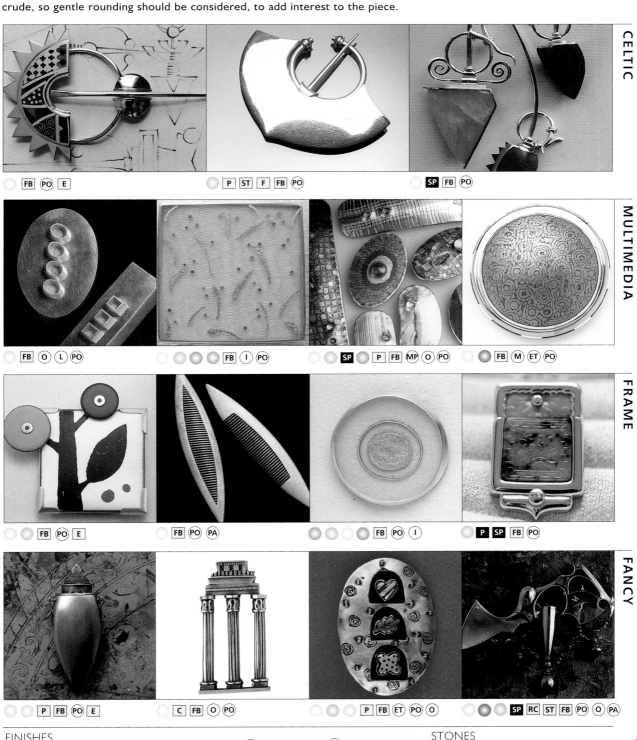

CELTIC

○ FB PO E   ○ P ST F FB PO   ○ SP FB PO

MULTIMEDIA

○ FB O L PO   ○○○ FB I PO   ○○ SP ○ P FB MP O PO   ○● FB M ET PO

FRAME

○○○ FB PO E   ○ FB PO PA   ○○○○○ FB PO I   ○ P SP FB PO

FANCY

○○ P FB PO E   ○ C FB O PO   ○○○ P FB ET PO O   ○○● SP RC ST FB PO O PA

43

WRIST & ARM PIECES

The way in which a wrist piece is worn is, to a degree, dictated by the wearer: if the form and circumference size permit, the piece may be passed over the elbow and up the arm to be worn as an arm piece, or, more traditionally, it may be worn on the wrist. The weight of a wrist piece will affect the way in which it sits. The heaviest section of the piece will be inclined to fall under the wrist, so there may be a need to balance the piece appropriately, to ensure that

OPEN

A wrist piece with an open form can be worn without passing over the hand, thus avoiding any difficulties that may occur if the hand of the wearer is disproportionately larger than his or her wrist.

FB PO

FB PO

HINGED

The fabrication of hinges is generally technically complex. Further, because of their small size, they can be quite delicate. Nonetheless, the hinge can be a very useful fitting, as it allows a piece to be fitted closer to the wearer's wrist or arm.

FB PO

FB PO

EXPANDING

Expansion in wrist pieces allows for greater flexibility, bypassing any potential sizing problems. Expandable pieces are also more versatile, in that they can be worn as either a wrist piece or an armlet.

FB PO

FW FB PO

FANCY

The weight of a piece must be considered so that it sits properly on the wrist, and to ensure the visibility of any focal points. Any vulnerable elements, such as stones or enamelling, will require protection.

FB PO

RC FB PO

44

MATERIALS

- gold
- silver
- platinum
- copper
- brass
- gilding metal
- nickel
- pewter
- steel
- titanium & aluminum
- organic
- plastic

PROCESSES/TECHNIQUES

- FB fabrication
- FW fretwork
- F forging
- P pressing
- RC repoussé & chasing
- C casting
- ST special techniques
- E enamelling

the detail sits in the desired position. If a wrist piece is designed to expand, the material or jointing must be strong enough to withstand the expansion without losing its original form. Hinged pieces can be technically challenging to fabricate, as there are a number of technical aspects to consider. The hinge itself must be made accurately, and it must be strong. Further, a hinge on a wrist piece often requires a catch, which can be difficult to fit accurately.

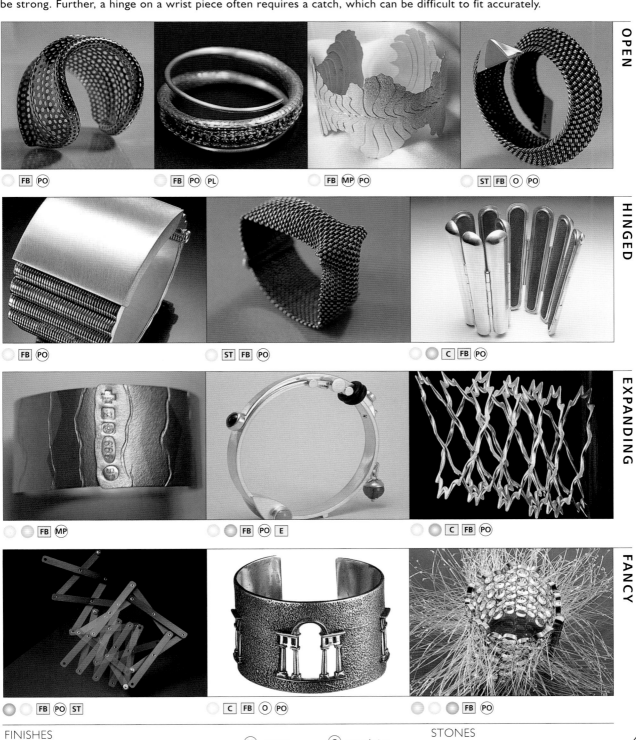

OPEN

○ FB PO

○ FB PO PL

○ FB MP PO

○ ST FB O PO

HINGED

○ FB PO

○ ST FB PO

○ ○ C FB PO

EXPANDING

○ ○ FB MP

○ ○ FB PO E

○ ○ C FB PO

FANCY

○ ○ FB PO ST

○ ○ C FB O PO

○ ○ ○ FB PO

45

BANGLES

The bangle is generally seen as a rigid form, although it may have articulated elements to facilitate fitting. The physical form that a bangle takes may vary from a hearty, solid piece that is tough enough to withstand daily wear, to hollow pieces that are vulnerable to knocks. The aperture of a bangle may need to be varied according to the size of the wearer. Both solid and hollow bangles are likely to suffer wear, so stones and materials that are soft or brittle should

SIMPLE

The simple bangle that is clean in both form and design can be satisfying in its purity. Simple forms can often be surprisingly difficult to fabricate, because there are generally fewer details to mask blemishes.

FB PO

F FB PO

HINGED

Hinges on bangles must be fabricated to be strong and durable. The section in which the hinge is positioned cannot be too deep or solid, or the hinge will not be able to open up properly.

P FB PO

FB PO

UNUSUAL

The bangle can be fabricated on a more extravagant scale than most jewelry forms; in particular, the form lends itself to sculptural designs. However, care should always be taken so that the function of the piece is not compromised by the demands of its design.

FB PO

FB PO

FANCY

Because of the way in which a bangle is worn, it is likely to suffer scrapes from movements of the arm and the use of the wrist. It is thus necessary to ensure that all areas are robust enough to withstand this treatment.

FW FB PO

FB PO

MATERIALS

- gold
- silver
- platinum
- copper
- brass
- gilding metal
- nickel
- pewter
- steel
- titanium & aluminum
- organic
- plastic

PROCESSES/TECHNIQUES

| FB | fabrication | F | forging | RC | repoussé & chasing | ST | special techniques |
| FW | fretwork | P | pressing | C | casting | E | enamelling |

be avoided; enamel is also inadvisable. The bangle is a versatile jewelry form in terms of its fabrication potential—it can be made large in size and bold in style, to create a strong visual impact. On a physical level, a bangle can give an impression of value if the weight is sympathetic to the form; if a large, hollow form is too light, it may lack the appeal of the same piece with a heavier feel.

SIMPLE

○ ○ F FB O PO

○ ● P FB PO

○ ○ FB MP

HINGED

○ ○ ST FB O PO

● FB ET PO PA

○ ○ FB PO

UNUSUAL

○ ST PO PL

○ ● FB PO

○ FB PO

FANCY

○ FB PO

○ ● ST FB PO

○ ○ F FB PO

BRACELETS

The overall form of a bracelet can be severely compromised by crude linking. To avoid a tacked-together effect, it is necessary to consider the way in which the forms will link as integral to the piece. The use of plain jump rings should be avoided where possible, as they can appear crude. Bracelets tend to be highly articulated forms, relying upon numerous or repeated links for flexibility. Linked units will inevitably suffer from mechanical wear at the joints. To

SIMPLE

With bracelets, visual simplicity tends to indicate technical simplicity. Fine linking detail should be avoided, as snagging is likely to occur, and finer bracelets may thus be damaged.

| C | FB | PO |

| C | FB | PO |

HINGED

Hinged bracelets tend not to be as flexible as bracelets that use other means of linking. They have restricted movement, generally working in one plane only, and are challenging to make accurately.

| FB | PO |

| P | FB | PO |

STONE-SET

Stones can be used to add highlights, color, and visual impact to bracelets. Because of potential wear, stones require protection; this can be achieved in a variety of innovative ways, including the addition of granulation or detail around the edge of the stone.

| C | FB | PO |

| FB | PO |

FANCY

Details in bracelets may be vulnerable due to the likelihood of knocks, scrapes, and snagging. Links are constantly wearing against each other, so frequently worn bracelets may eventually suffer damage, and need repair work.

| FB | PO |

| FB | PO |

MATERIALS

- gold
- silver
- platinum
- copper
- brass
- gilding metal
- nickel
- pewter
- steel
- titanium & aluminum
- organic
- plastic

PROCESSES/TECHNIQUES

| FB | fabrication | F | forging | RC | repoussé & chasing | ST | special techniques |
| FW | fretwork | P | pressing | C | casting | E | enamelling |

minimize this type of damage, ensure, where possible, that each of the links are equally weighted, and that they are made from the same material; a heavier section will wear a finer one, and a harder material will wear a softer one. Catches should be simple to handle, yet strong and secure. A variety of sizing options can be included with a toggle catch; this can be achieved by adding two or more eyelets through which the bar can pass to close the bracelet.

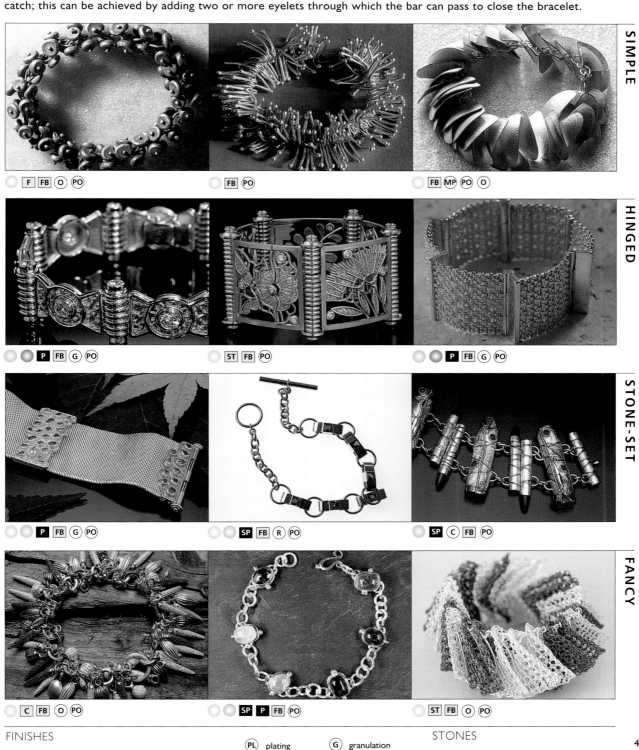

SIMPLE

◯ F FB ◯ PO   ◯ FB PO   ◯ FB MP PO O

HINGED

◯ ◯ P FB G PO   ◯ ST FB PO   ◯ ◯ P FB G PO

STONE-SET

◯ ◯ P FB G PO   ◯ ◯ SP FB R PO   ◯ SP C FB PO

FANCY

◯ C FB ◯ PO   ◯ ◯ SP P FB PO   ◯ ST FB ◯ PO

FINISHES

◯ PO polish   ET etching   R reticulation   PL plating   ◯ oxidizing   G granulation
MP mill pressing   EN engraving   L leaf or foil   PA patination   M mokumé gane
                                                                                    I inlay

STONES

P precious   O organic
SP semiprecious   S synthetic & other

49

RINGS • BANDS

Band rings are generally a good choice for everyday wear because they tend to have little or no excessive extruding detail, making them generally easy to live with. Stone-set bands have become a popular choice in contemporary jewelry for engagement rings, as they are able to withstand the rigors of a modern lifestyle more readily than other ring forms. Many wedding bands and engagement rings do not sit well together, so the fit of the two forms should be

PARALLEL BANDS

It is easier to pass a narrow parallel band over a knuckle than a wide one. Indeed, a wide band may need to be made at least a size larger than a narrow one to fit over the same finger. Remember that temperature affects finger size.

ST FB PO   FB PO   ST FB PO

TAPERED BANDS

Tapering can be used to draw attention to a focal point, and to reduce both visual and material weight. Tapering a wide ring to a narrow base can also be a method of reducing potential discomfort to the wearer.

C FB PO   C FB PO   C FB PO

FREE-FORM

Varying a band's profile can add complexity, variety, and visual interest to the piece. If the band's shape is such that one section is heavier than the rest of it, the distribution of the weight should be considered if the band is meant to be worn in a particular way.

C FB PO   C FB PO   C FB PO

STONE-SET

Stones set in rings can be subject to a great deal of wear, and can be vulnerable to damage; the choice of stone and setting should thus be carefully considered. The depth of the stone may dictate the thickness of the band.

FB I PO   C FB PO   C FB PO EN

MATERIALS

 gold
 silver
 platinum
 copper
brass
gilding metal
 nickel
 pewter
 steel
 titanium & aluminum
 organic
 plastic

PROCESSES/TECHNIQUES

FB fabrication   F forging   RC repoussé & chasing   ST special techniques
FW fretwork   P pressing   C casting   E enamelling

considered from the outset if wearing them together is desired. Polishing the inside of a ring and softening its inner edges with a gentle curve will help it pass over the knuckle more easily, and will ensure greater comfort for the wearer. Take care to avoid sharp edges on the inside of the ring. Hollowed out bands can trap soap behind them, which can lead to skin irritation; it may thus be advisable to remove them before washing one's hands.

PARALLEL BANDS

○ ○ C FB PO   ● P FB PO   ○ ○ FB PO   ○ C F PO

TAPERED BANDS

○ P C FB PO EN   ○ ○ FB R PO   ○ ○ ● P FB PO   ○ SP FB PO

FREE-FORM

○ C FB PO O   ○ ○ FB PO   ○ ST PO

STONE-SET

○ P RC PO   ○ P C FB PO   ○ SP C FB PO   ○ SP C FB PO EN

FINISHES

PO polish
MP mill pressing
ET etching
EN engraving
R reticulation
L leaf or foil
PL plating
O oxidizing
PA patination
G granulation
M mokumé gane
I inlay

STONES

P precious
SP semiprecious
O organic
S synthetic & other

51

Stone-set rings tend to be regarded as precious, although many are set with semiprecious stones that simply add color and interest, with no great cost. Softer stones are not recommended for rings that will be subject to hard daily wear, as the stone may be easily scratched. Large stone settings in engagement rings—as would be necessary for a large solitaire, or for clusters in a fine shank—may not sit naturally or parallel with a wedding band, so the desirability of

SOLITAIRE

An embedded solitaire stone will need to be set in a section of the shank that is as deep as the stone, to prevent the apex from digging into the flesh. Claw settings that hold a valuable stone should be checked regularly.

FB PO

C FB PO

FB PO

GROUP

Stones that are positioned and set in a group to surround a feature are likely to be vulnerable, so both the stones and the setting must be suitably strong. Where possible, a hard material such as platinum should be used for claws, and for setting valuable stones.

FB PO

FB PO

C FB PO

ROW

The number and size of stones in a full eternity band can be a factor in determining the ring's size. The depth of the shank in which the stones are to be embedded will need to be as deep as the deepest stone.

ST FB PO

FB PO

C FB PO

FANCY

If a combination of settings, stones, and cuts is to be used, take care to ensure that any vulnerable stones or settings are adequately protected from wear. The use of harder materials for these elements is advisable.

FB PO

FB PO

FB PO

MATERIALS

- gold
- silver
- platinum
- copper
- brass
- gilding metal
- nickel
- pewter
- steel
- titanium & aluminum
- organic
- plastic

PROCESSES/TECHNIQUES

FB fabrication	F forging
FW fretwork	P pressing

RC repoussé & chasing	ST special techniques
C casting	E enamelling

wearing the two pieces together should be considered. Because claws are relatively vulnerable due to their small size, a claw setting can wear fairly quickly, and so it will need to be checked regularly. The fewer the number of claws the setting is reliant upon, the more frequently the ring should be checked. Excessive changes to the size of a ring may affect the shape of the setting, and can cause stones to crack or drop out.

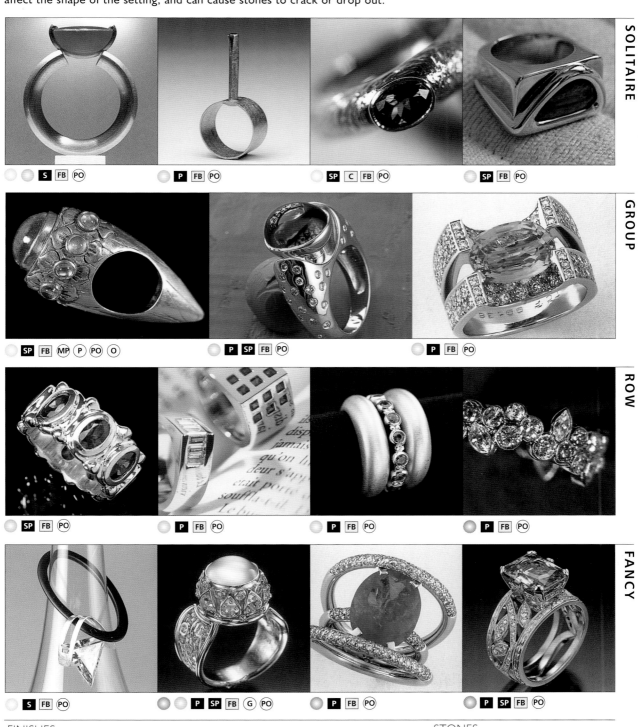

FINISHES

STONES

53

(PO) polish	(ET) etching	(R) reticulation
(MP) mill pressing	(EN) engraving	(L) leaf or foil

(PL) plating
(O) oxidizing
(PA) patination

(G) granulation
(M) mokumé gane
(I) inlay

P precious	O organic
SP semiprecious	S synthetic & other

The ring form is tremendously versatile, despite the limitations of its size. Indeed, the relatively small size of a ring has its advantages: there is a clear limit to the amount of work that can done on a ring, as well as a limit to the material content, and therefore the material cost (excluding stones, where there is virtually no price ceiling). Ring forms and sizes can vary tremendously; wide rings will displace a greater area of flesh, and will therefore need to be a larger size

FREE-FORM
Ring forms that are apparently structured or symmetrical can often be easily fashioned by wax carving for casting, and generally possess great character.

C · FB · PO   C · FB · PO   C · FB · PO

FRIVOLOUS
A ring can take many frivolous forms. It can comprise a narrative, telling a story through its design; it can be a folly, with a light-hearted theme; or it may follow a fashionable trend. Highly sculptural ring forms can also be made frivolous.

FB · PO   C · FB · PO   C · FB · PO

MULTIMEDIA
The mixing of metals has become more popular in contemporary design, and reflects the current tendency to wear a mixture of gold and silver at the same time. Other materials may also be included, to add color and interest.

FB · PO   C · FB · PO   C · FB · PO

FEATURE
While most rings have focal points that can be seen as features, a special effort can be made to spotlight a certain aspect of a piece, such as a stone or a design element, calling attention to it as the definitive feature.

C · FB · PO   C · FB · PO   FB · PO

MATERIALS

- gold
- silver
- platinum
- copper
- brass
- gilding metal
- nickel
- pewter
- steel
- titanium & aluminum
- organic
- plastic

PROCESSES/TECHNIQUES

| FB | fabrication | F | forging | RC | repoussé & chasing | ST | special techniques |
| FW | fretwork | P | pressing | C | casting | E | enamelling |

than a narrower one meant for the same finger. Rings can have a variety of functions, from the decorative to the symbolic. They can be seen as suggestive of social standing; for example, signet rings in Britain can be read to imply that the wearer has wealth and property, while in North America, college rings suggest a higher education. A ring can also take on significance when it is handed down through generations of a family as an heirloom.

FREE-FORM

FB PO   FB PO   P FB PO   F FB PO

FRIVOLOUS

C FB PO   FB PO O   SP S P FB PO   FB PO

MULTIMEDIA

FB PO ST   FB PO O   P FB PO   SP FB PO

FEATURE

FB PO   SP C FB EN PO   SP FB PO   SP ST F P FB PO

FINISHES

PO polish
MP mill pressing
ET etching
EN engraving
R reticulation
L leaf or foil
PL plating
O oxidizing
PA patination
G granulation
M mokumé gane
I inlay

STONES

P precious
SP semiprecious
O organic
S synthetic & other

55

Rings can be hard to label specifically, as they often contain features that can be defined in numerous ways, and thus can fall into multiple categories. They are perhaps the most easily worn type of jewelry form; they can be adorned without the aid of a mirror, as is often not the case with such items as earrings and brooches. Another advantage of the ring form is that its fabrication is an individual affair, and thus is not subject to problems involving the matching of

SIMPLE

Simple ring forms are particularly useful for functional or symbolic rings, such as the signet ring. Simple rings can also be more versatile, and may appear as unisex pieces rather than gender-specific ones.

C FB PO

FB PO

FB PO

ORGANIC

The use of organic materials and forms can add great interest and character to a piece, whereas pieces that rely on man-made materials and processes for fabrication can lack individuality.

C FB PO

C FB PO ET

C FB PO

ARTICULATED

Articulated rings add interest with their capacity for movement. Joints may be delicate, so care may be necessary when such pieces are worn. The joints should be made from a suitably strong, durable material.

ST FB PO

C FB PO

FB PO EN

FANCY

Any unexpected or unusual features in a ring can add excitement and interest to the piece. A ring that challenges the preconceptions of form or function, even slightly, can be visually stimulating.

FB PO

FB PO

P FB PO

MATERIALS

- gold
- silver
- platinum
- copper
- brass
- gilding metal
- nickel
- pewter
- steel
- titanium & aluminum
- organic
- plastic

PROCESSES/TECHNIQUES

| FB | fabrication | F | forging | RC | repoussé & chasing | ST | special techniques |
| FW | fretwork | P | pressing | C | casting | E | enamelling |

multiple forms. Rings can be problematic, however, in that the necessity of creating different sizes for different wearers can make production difficult—not to mention potentially costly. Extreme enlargement and reduction of ring sizes will often result in the distortion of a detail, or of the general form. Further, stones may need to be removed for sizing, as few can take the heat of soldering, and the physical stress caused by hammering and forming.

SIMPLE

○ SP C FB PO   ○ P FB PO   ○ SP F FB PO   ○ ○ FB O PO

ORGANIC

○ ○ FB PO O   ○ ○ F FB PO   ○ SP FB R PO

ARTICULATED

○ ○ SP S FB PO   ○ C FB PO   ○ S FB PO   ○ ○ ○ ST FB PO

FANCY

○ S FB ST PO   ○ S C FB PO PL   ○ C FB PO   ○ P SP FB PO

FINISHES

- PO polish
- MP mill pressing
- ET etching
- EN engraving
- R reticulation
- L leaf or foil
- PL plating
- O oxidizing
- PA patination
- G granulation
- M mokumé gane
- I inlay

STONES

- P precious
- SP semiprecious
- O organic
- S synthetic & other

57

CUFFLINKS

Cufflinks are a popular form of masculine jewelry, having both decorative and practical functions. They can be subject to wear, and occasionally to unwelcome pressure if they are leaned upon. Solid bars will be vulnerable under pressure if the bar is not sufficiently strong, or if either of the soldered joints is weak. Chains and two-part link fittings tend to be easier to repair if they involve enamelling or if they are stone-set, as their parts can be more readily broken down,

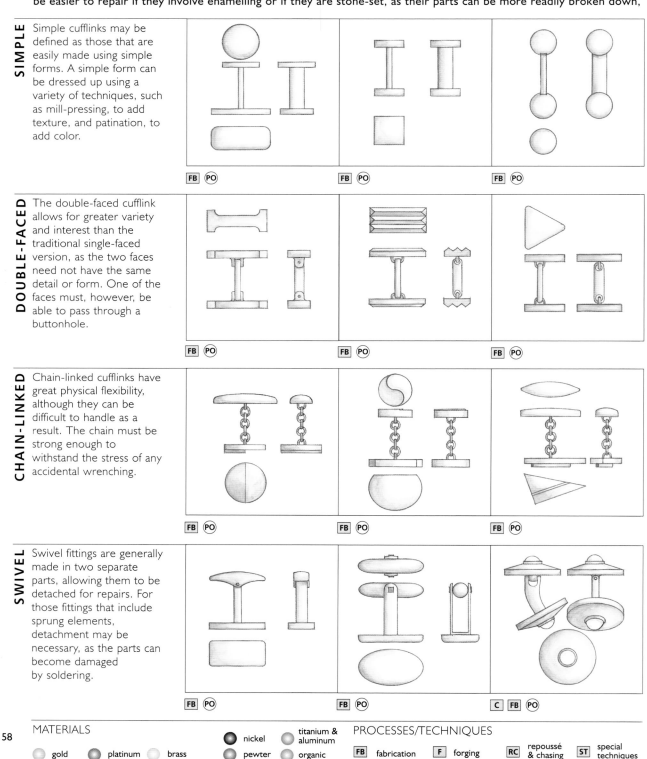

SIMPLE

Simple cufflinks may be defined as those that are easily made using simple forms. A simple form can be dressed up using a variety of techniques, such as mill-pressing, to add texture, and patination, to add color.

FB PO FB PO FB PO

DOUBLE-FACED

The double-faced cufflink allows for greater variety and interest than the traditional single-faced version, as the two faces need not have the same detail or form. One of the faces must, however, be able to pass through a buttonhole.

FB PO FB PO FB PO

CHAIN-LINKED

Chain-linked cufflinks have great physical flexibility, although they can be difficult to handle as a result. The chain must be strong enough to withstand the stress of any accidental wrenching.

FB PO FB PO FB PO

SWIVEL

Swivel fittings are generally made in two separate parts, allowing them to be detached for repairs. For those fittings that include sprung elements, detachment may be necessary, as the parts can become damaged by soldering.

FB PO FB PO C FB PO

58

MATERIALS

- ○ gold
- ○ silver
- ● platinum
- ● copper
- ○ brass
- ○ gilding metal
- ● nickel
- ● pewter
- ● steel
- ○ titanium & aluminum
- ○ organic
- ○ plastic

PROCESSES/TECHNIQUES

| FB | fabrication | F | forging | RC | repoussé & chasing | ST | special techniques |
| FW | fretwork | P | pressing | C | casting | E | enamelling |

thus avoiding damage from any necessary soldering. Swivel fittings are technically difficult to make, but commercial versions can be easily purchased, and are a relatively good value, even when the cost of manufacture is taken into consideration. Three-part swivel fittings, where the body attaches to the form with a joint part, are preferable to two-part swivel fittings with rigid arms, as arms can be more easily broken.

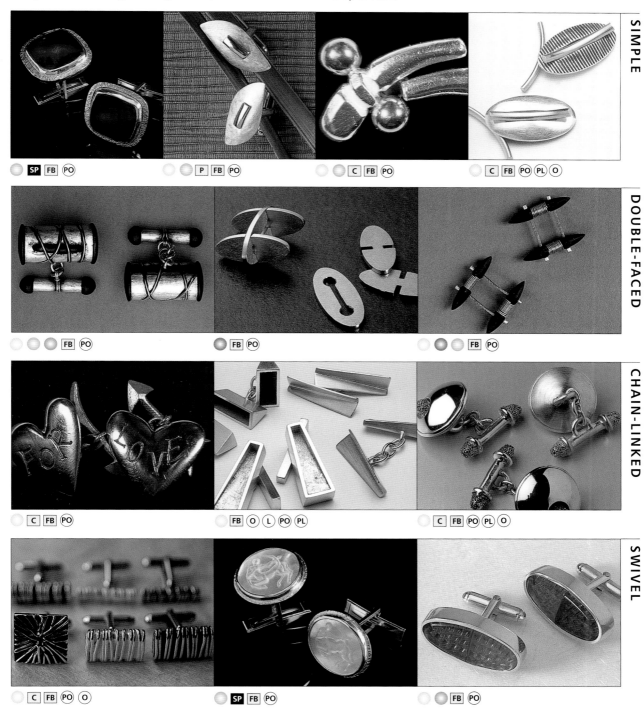

SIMPLE

SP FB PO

P FB PO

C FB PO

C FB PO PL O

DOUBLE-FACED

FB PO

FB PO

FB PO

CHAIN-LINKED

C FB PO

FB O L PO PL

C FB PO PL O

SWIVEL

C FB PO O

SP FB PO

FB PO

FINISHES

PO polish
MP mill pressing
ET etching
EN engraving
R reticulation
L leaf or foil
PL plating
O oxidizing
PA patination
G granulation
M mokumé gane
I inlay

STONES

P precious
SP semiprecious
O organic
S synthetic & other

The availability of men's jewelry tends to be subject to the whims of fashion. A more traditional form of men's jewelry, dress studs continue to be an integral part of a man's formal evening dress. They have remained generally classical in form, and, because of their enduring popularity, they are easier to find than most other varieties of men's jewelry. There is little that defines a ring as being specifically for a man, but, generally speaking, bold, strong forms are more

SIMPLE RINGS

Most men's rings are simple in form and design, and are capable of withstanding the rough treatment they are likely to receive during daily wear. Signet rings and wedding bands are the most commonly worn types of rings for men.

C FB PO

FB PO

C FB PO

OTHER RINGS

In the past, men tended to wear jewelry as an exhibition of status. Men's fashion has become less serious and more daring in the past decade, and thus flamboyant rings are now seen with greater frequency in contemporary men's jewelry.

FB PO

C FB PO

C FB PO

PINS & STUDS

The backs on dress studs can be screw-fit, fixed, or they may have a detachable clasp. If the backs are fixed, it is necessary to ensure that they will be able to pass through the buttonholes of a dress shirt, which are generally small.

FB PO

FB PO

FB PO

ASSORTED

There are currently few popular forms of men's jewelry beyond cufflinks and rings. Although somewhat out of fashion at the moment, it is still possible to find tie slides. Sets of jewelry can be appealing if a bolder statement is desired.

FB PO

RC FB PO

FB PO

MATERIALS

- gold
- silver
- platinum
- copper
- brass
- gilding metal
- nickel
- pewter
- steel
- titanium & aluminum
- organic
- plastic

PROCESSES/TECHNIQUES

- **FB** fabrication
- **FW** fretwork
- **F** forging
- **P** pressing
- **RC** repoussé & chasing
- **C** casting
- **ST** special techniques
- **E** enamelling

likely to attract a male audience. Another popular piece of jewelry for men is the decorative pin. Similar in appearance to a small brooch, pins tend to be figurative or symbolic rather than solely decorative when worn by men, although they may not have been intended as gender-specific when made. Like the AIDS Awareness red ribbon, the best symbolic pins are simple and easily wearable, while conveying their messages clearly at the same time.

SIMPLE RINGS

○ ● ○ ST FB PO   ○ C FB PO   ○ C FB PO

OTHER RINGS

○ SP C FB PO   ○ ○ ● FB PO   ○ C FB PO   ○ FB PO

PINS & STUDS

○ ○ C FB PO PA   ○ C FB PO   ○ C FB PO   ○ ○ C FB PO

ASSORTED

○ SP FB G PO   ○ FB PO   ○ ○ FB PO O   ○ ● ○ FB PO

FINISHES

(PO) polish   (ET) etching   (R) reticulation   (PL) plating   (G) granulation
(MP) mill pressing   (EN) engraving   (L) leaf or foil   (O) oxidizing   (M) mokumé gane
                                                                      (PA) patination   (I) inlay

STONES

P precious   **O** organic
SP semiprecious   **S** synthetic & other

61

BEADS

The bead is one of the oldest forms of jewelry. It can be used as the focal point of a piece, or assembled in combination with other beads or fittings to make earrings, necklaces, bracelets, or rings. Beads are generally strung through a single hole that allows the bead to turn freely, and be viewed all the way around its circumference. To restrict a bead so that it cannot turn readily, two holes can be used to string through in place of a single hole. Beads

SIMPLE

Simple beads can benefit from subtle detailing in their form, surface texture, or color. Such details can be created by mill pressing, etching, patination, or piercing. Colored thread can also be used to enliven beading.

ST FB PO   P FB PO   P FB PO

ORGANIC

Beads need not be fabricated as multiples; the use of a variety of processes and organic materials can lend a sense of character and individuality to each bead. Forms and detailing may be inspired by the organic element.

FB ET G PO   C FB PO   F FB PO

VARIOUS

A bead can be fabricated as the single focal point for a piece of jewelry. Techniques such as engraving can be used to create fine detail, which suits the form well. Casting can be used to produce multiple beads of the same form.

FB ET PO   FW FB PO   FB PO EN

FANCY

Fancy forms may indicate a specific function, or require a particular direction for wear. Ornate beads can have scratchy details that may cause irritation to skin, so consider a smooth finish if possible.

FB PO   ST FB PO   FB PO

MATERIALS

- gold
- silver
- platinum
- copper
- brass
- gilding metal
- nickel
- pewter
- steel
- titanium & aluminum
- organic
- plastic

PROCESSES/TECHNIQUES

| FB | fabrication | F | forging | RC | repoussé & chasing | ST | special techniques |
| FW | fretwork | P | pressing | C | casting | E | enamelling |

tend to be strung on thread, and the places where the thread enters and exits the bead may eventually become frayed. To protect against fraying, soften and polish all entry and exit points, and avoid sharp or serrated edges. If a hollow bead has a thin edge, solder a small jump ring around the hole; this will add depth to and soften the hole. Knotting the thread in between the beads can limit loss if breakage occurs, and will lengthen the overall piece.

SIMPLE

○ SP F FB PO

○ ○ FB PO

○ ○ SP FB PO

ORGANIC

○ S F FB PO O

○ SP S F FB PO O

○ ○ ST FB PO PA

VARIOUS

○ SP S O FB PO

○ ○ O SP FB PO

○ SP P FB MP PO

FANCY

○ ○ SP P FB PO E

○ ○ ○ F FB PO L

○ ○ ST FB PO O

FINISHES

(PO) polish   (ET) etching   (R) reticulation

(MP) mill pressing   (EN) engraving   (L) leaf or foil

(PL) plating   (G) granulation

(O) oxidizing   (M) mokumé gane

(PA) patination   (I) inlay

STONES

P precious   O organic

SP semiprecious   S synthetic & other

63

CHAINS

Because chains are generally a series of repeated links of the same configuration, they can be made to any length. However, hand-made chains may have graduated links that can define the length. Because the units in a chain may twist when assembled, the creation of a prototype may be prudent in order to highlight any potential problems, and so that the master pattern can be adjusted if necessary. Kinking is another likely problem; barreling the chain can help

SIMPLE

Simple chains tend to have links that are close together, with each repeated section being relatively short. The longer the length of each individual section, the less flexible the overall chain will appear.

FB PO   C FB PO   FB PO

FREE-FORM

Some chains may appear to be unconventional because the individual forms do not look like traditional chain links. However, so long as the units are made so that they can repeat to an infinite length, the piece will, by definition, be considered a chain.

FB PO   C FB PO   FB PO

CAST

Casting is a useful process for making chain links, although cast links can make the overall chain quite heavy. The fabrication of cast links typically involves casting them first as a solid form. They are then cut open, joined, and, finally, re-soldered after assembly.

C FB PO   C FB PO   C FB PO

FANCY

If the links in a chain are too complex or highly detailed, there may be a problem with the movement of the piece. The weight of one or more of the links may be used as a device to ensure that the piece lies in a specific direction.

C FB PO   C FB PO   FB PO

MATERIALS

gold	platinum	brass	nickel	titanium & aluminum
silver	copper	gilding metal	pewter	organic
			steel	plastic

PROCESSES/TECHNIQUES

FB	fabrication	F	forging	RC	repoussé & chasing	ST	special techniques
FW	fretwork	P	pressing	C	casting	E	enamelling

to wear the joints so that they move freely. Alternatively, metal polish rubbed on the links will help them wear gently and work more freely. Although the links in a chain will likely all wear down at some point, they will not necessarily all wear down at the same time, and thus the chain may need to be repaired repeatedly. Avoid hard links joining soft ones and heavy links joining light ones, as this will cause the weaker section to wear, and the chain is more likely to break.

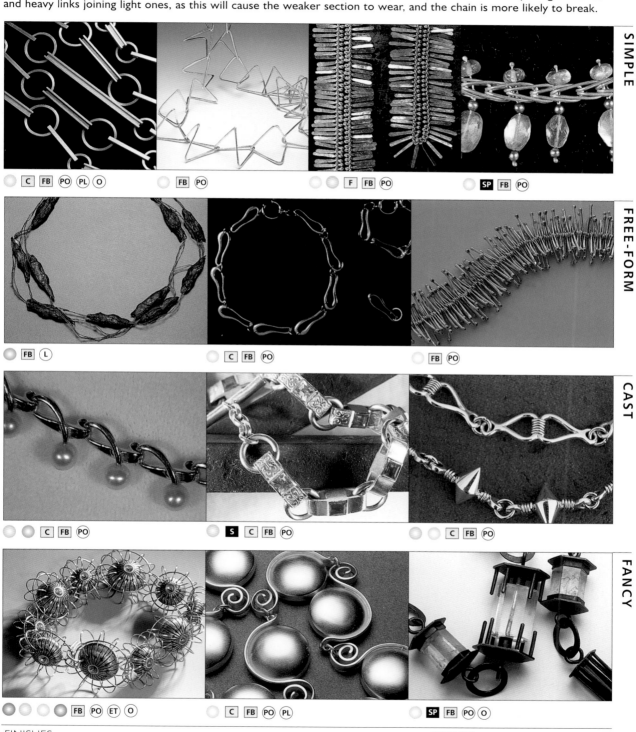

SIMPLE

◯ C FB PO PL O   ◯ FB PO   ◯ ◯ F FB PO   ◯ SP FB PO

FREE-FORM

◯ FB L   ◯ C FB PO   ◯ FB PO

CAST

◯ ◯ C FB PO   ◯ S C FB PO   ◯ ◯ C FB PO

FANCY

◯ ◯ ◯ ◯ FB PO ET O   ◯ C FB PO PL   ◯ SP FB PO O

FINISHES

				STONES		
PO polish	ET etching	R reticulation	PL plating	O oxidizing	G granulation	
MP mill pressing	EN engraving	L leaf or foil	PA patination	I inlay	M mokumé gane	

STONES

P precious   O organic
SP semiprecious   S synthetic & other

65

The word "suite" describes a set of two or more jewelry pieces that are related to each other in any number of ways. A suite can take the form of a traditional set of jewelry, such as a set of engagement or wedding rings, or it could be a collection of different but related pieces. A suite might also take a more unusual form; for example, a set of jewelry in which the various components can function independently, but when viewed or worn together, are seen as a whole.

Suites

A collection of brightly colored anodized aluminum pins.

Three figures cavort in different poses, but clearly belong to the same family of brooches.

One of the most common types of jewelry suites is that which consists of a necklace and earrings. This format tends to conjure up an image of fine jewelry and a formal occasion, for which a matching set of jewels may be required. Nowadays, however, there is less demand for matching jewelry; the imaginative combining of favorite pieces is a more often seen alternative.

In department stores, we usually see suites showcased as a collection of jewelry forms that have been made by the same jeweler. There may be continuity in the set of materials that link the pieces, or a repeated motif that acts as the visual thread between them, so that there is a "family" feel to the grouping—even if the forms vary dramatically.

The fashion collection showcased in a store will typically be made up of pieces that tempt us to buy more than just a single item; a wide choice of jewelry forms are commonly included, from rings, earrings, and brooches to bracelets and neckpieces. The overall effect is designed to draw us in and dazzle us, using the larger featured pieces as the eye-catching components.

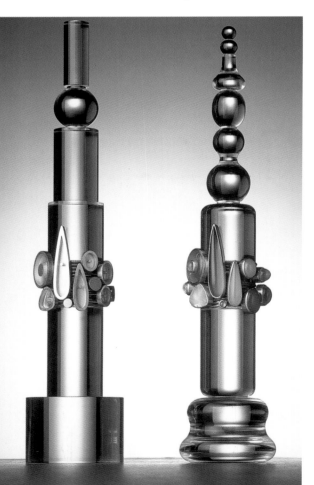

Two lathe-turned stands are integral to these sets of gold and jeweled rings.

A trio of brooches of the same form are individualized with different details.

Cornelian coral and gold are coupled in a traditional set of jewelry.

These three brooches suggest a storyline, connecting them to form a narrative suite.

Swirling motifs unite these pieces as a collection.

The jeweler may see the suite as a series that develops and explores a theme. By expanding on a single idea through varying the configuration, size, form, color, material, or finish, for example, a series can become a collection that represents a cohesive body of work.

A particular technique may serve as an inspiration for a suite of jewelry, in that it allows for the easy repetition of a common form, while another element—the surface detail, for example—can be changed without losing the common thread between the pieces. Pressing and casting are particularly good techniques for this way of working, and more contemporary processes, such as photoetching and electroforming, are also useful methods for reproduction.

For some jewelers, the use of a particular form, configuration, or device is a "signature" of their work. Any forms that encompass new ideas along with this signature may constitute a new direction for the work, and might be considered a new collection.

A suite can be treated as a collection of pieces that make up a three-dimensional canvas, where an overall story may be told. When assembled off the body, individual pieces can become part of a sculpture. Where there are a number of pieces which can be worn in a variety of combinations, the wearer is given the power to decide how to assemble the pieces on the body.

Whatever form the suite takes, the relationship that exists between the pieces adds interest and visual attraction to the ensemble, and provides us with the opportunity to explore and enjoy the relationship between the forms.

Articulated silver rings with semiprecious stones make a cohesive statement.

Throughout history, jewelers have reflected the influences of culture and convention by the inclusion of popular motifs in jewelry design. Some motifs have become so well-known that they typify an era. In Egyptian jewelry, for example, the portrayal of a scarab was the height of fashion; the scarab seen in jewelry today still evokes that ancient culture.

At various points throughout history, jewelry motifs reflected the social position of the wearer; the wearing of magical, ecclesiastical, and devotional jewelry are examples of this fashion. Today, the cross is rarely worn as a significant religious statement, although it has survived as a decorative form.

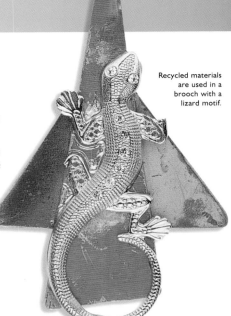

Recycled materials are used in a brooch with a lizard motif.

Motifs

A silver pin with an airplane motif.

Motifs can map social change, as jewelry forms reflect the continuous flux between cultures; this can be seen in the growing or waning use of specific motifs. In western jewelry, the growing presence of the oriental symbol of "yin and yang" indicates the increasing interest and presence of eastern influences and spirituality in western culture. Similarly, political motifs such as the "peace" symbol found their way into jewelry design as the nuclear threat became a high-profile issue, much as the Tudor rose was used in its day.

This brooch poses the question: Which came first, the chicken or the egg?

The frogs climb the wearer in this three-brooch set.

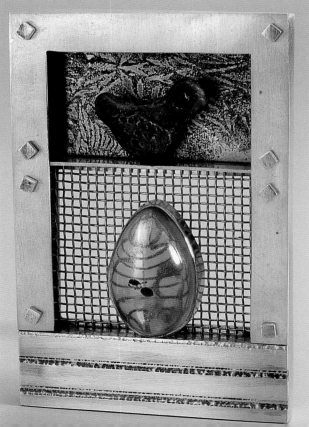

Over the years, themes such as love have been consistently celebrated using motifs. The use of the heart shape to symbolize the sentiment of love, affection, and feelings of devotion is practically as enduring as the emotion itself. From friendship rings to fashion jewelry, the heart shape has graced jewelry forms for centuries in the form of a token to celebrate relationships and unions. From such important life events as engagement and marriage to the ever-more popular Valentine's Day, there are many opportunities for the heart shape to make an appearance in jewelry. Symbolically youthful and optimistic, the heart shape has managed to remain a firm favorite as a motif, and is likely to endure as such for the foreseeable future.

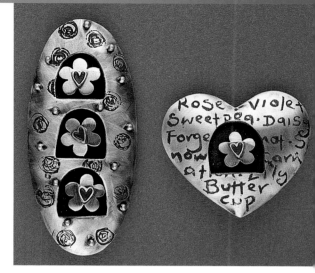

A pair of brooches include the heart as either form or detail.

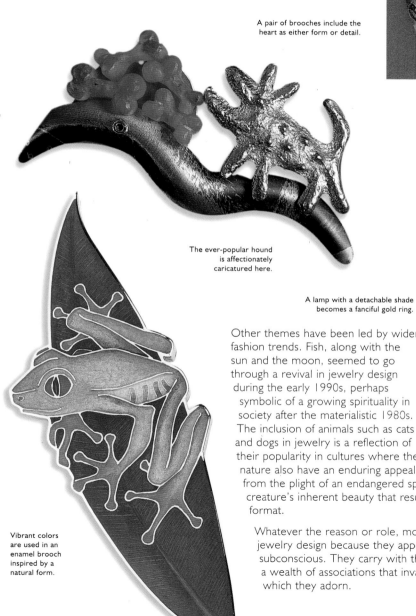

The ever-popular hound is affectionately caricatured here.

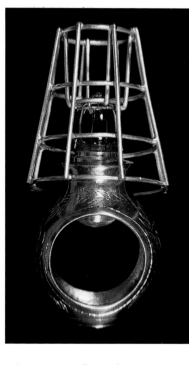

A lamp with a detachable shade becomes a fanciful gold ring.

Other themes have been led by wider fashion trends. Fish, along with the sun and the moon, seemed to go through a revival in jewelry design during the early 1990s, perhaps symbolic of a growing spirituality in society after the materialistic 1980s. The inclusion of animals such as cats and dogs in jewelry is a reflection of their popularity in cultures where they are kept as pets. Forms from nature also have an enduring appeal. Their popularity may derive from the plight of an endangered species, although more often it is a creature's inherent beauty that results in its portrayal in a jewelry format.

Whatever the reason or role, motifs play a significant part in jewelry design because they appeal to the conscious or subconscious. They carry with them their own history, and bring a wealth of associations that invariably enrich the jewelry forms which they adorn.

Vibrant colors are used in an enamel brooch inspired by a natural form.

Fashion jewelry has become a very popular area of the jewelry market. Historically, fashion jewelry was typically just imitation jewelry, mimicking, as the name suggests, the styles of jewelry that were desirable at the time. Today, fashion jewelry is a separate, distinct category of jewelry in its own right, and not just an imitation of the "real thing."

Fashion

An attention-seeking "bunny ears" ring made of silver and plastic.

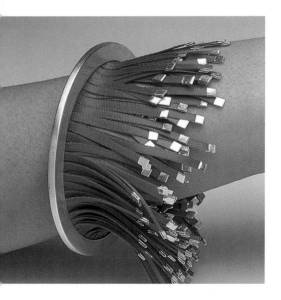

A silver and ribbon bangle attracts attention with bold color and movement.

Fashion jewelry is often produced by working a material that might be perceived to be of a lesser quality with sensitivity and style, thereby creating a sense of quality in a material not normally seen in a jewelry context. For example, a silver ring sprouting plastic horns studded with silver beads not only intimates quality—it also has great fashion appeal.

Ideas for styling fashion jewelry may begin by taking a fresh approach to established concepts, materials, images, or forms, and turning them on their heads so that they offer another view about the conventional. Simple objects can be used out of context in a way that has fashion appeal; for example, a toothbrush can become part of a jewelry form, deftly redefining the stone in a ring format, and catching the eye with the gloss and color of the brush head.

Just as a piece of clothing is made to move in a certain way when worn, so jewelry forms can be made to work with the body and the way it functions. In a bangle, red ribbons might flow from a simple band so that the movement of the wearer's wrist becomes a focal point. In such a design, ribbons are used to shadow the wrist's movement, while the sensation of the ribbons on the skin makes the piece a tactile experience for the wearer.

The fashion catwalk, where a sense of theater is necessary, is a fabulous showcase for dramatic jewelry. Larger pieces can be difficult to fit into an everyday context, but their visual impact can project an image so vivid that it evokes a scenario, such as a neckpiece that brims over with fauna and butterflies to conjure up a fairytale.

A collection of silver and gold rings makes a distinct statement.

The concepts of levity and play can also be useful tools for jewelry forms. For example, the concepts of restriction and freedom can be juxtaposed, so that a static, restrictive choker accentuates the movement and freedom of the attached pendants by contrast.

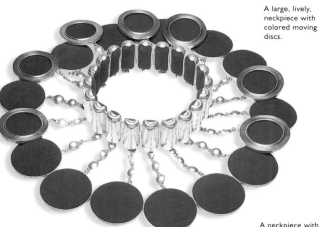

A large, lively, neckpiece with colored moving discs.

A neckpiece with sculptural silver forms and a mill-pressed finish.

The monetary value of a fashion piece need not be compromised for the sake of fashion.

Materials chosen for fashion jewelry often include semiprecious stones and silver. Materials typically associated with fine jewelry, such as gold and diamonds, can also be seen in pieces that could be defined as both fashion and fine jewelry. A necklace for the fashion market may have the hallmarks of a fine jewelry piece: costly materials, sculptural forms, and, of course, quality. A fashion necklace can also have the delicacy associated with fine jewelry; the fine strands of a delicate necklace, for example, may be punctuated with semiprecious stones and precious beads. Fashion ring forms are particularly likely to be made using precious materials, as they require only a small amount of the materials used, and so the cost does not become prohibitive.

A face-framing paper and silver collar.

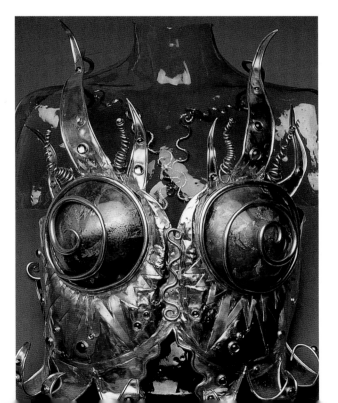

Whether the intrinsic value of fashion jewelry derives from its monetary value or from the value of the concept, fashion jewelry brings energy and fresh ideas to the jewelry form, keeping design spontaneous and responsive, and constantly exploring new propositions for jewelry with fashion appeal.

Bold, curvaceous, forms are used in these silver cufflinks.

Enamelling adds color to this gold-plated bustier.

An otherwise unwanted object, seen and then spirited away into a pocket to be held or hidden away later in a special place, has great appeal. Indeed, the compulsion inspired by found objects has much in common with the way that certain items of jewelry make us feel, so it is neither surprising nor unnatural that the two should be combined.

Found objects

A keyhole becomes figurative in a brooch where screws form a crown of hair.

Hazelnuts are used as the drops in a pair of silver hook earrings.

Some found objects are jewel-like already—seeds and nuts, for example, have a bead-like quality, and can be translated into the role of a bead with minimal effort. Other, harder, materials, such as stones and shells, can pose a greater challenge, because they may require diamond tools to work them, but the effort is generally worthwhile. Be it a hazelnut that conjures up memories of a relationship, or a pebble that sums up a sunny day on the beach, a found object can make the perfect complement for a simple earring hook or a delicate chain.

Electroformed twigs and precious stones are combined in this bangle collection.

Toothbrushes are taken out of their normal functional context and used to add color to jewelry pieces.

One example of a found stone that could be perceived as precious due to its relative inaccessibility is the meteorite. Its value as a found object may also lie in the emotions that it evokes for the wearer. For example, a piece of meteorite given to a partner or friend as a token of some sort redefines the concept of the stone, transforming it from an item of monetary value into one that has emotional value as well.

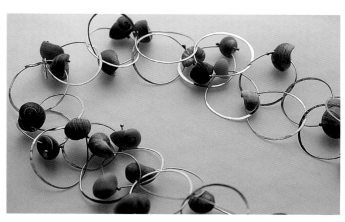

Fine silver hoops are adorned with tiny seashells to form a delicate chain.

Carefully selected pebbles are strung together with forged silver disks for a natural look.

Screws are used as claws to hold a stone in place on a wooden shank.

In our transient society, where so much is expendable, there is a growing interest in ecology and nature. Twigs set discreetly with diamonds, or seedpods with a flash of color peeping out from their mouths create a feeling of preciousness. Seedpods strung with a natural fiber may not have any traditionally precious materials as part of the form, yet they still exude the quality of a fine piece of jewelry.

Found objects can also be used to tell a story. This can be done by masking the typical associations we make of them and combining them with other objects, to create a completely different form. In this way, a keyhole paired with screws can be made into a face crowned by a wild head of hair.

Fashioning found materials into a jewelry form is a time-honored tradition—ebony and ivory have been fashioned for centuries, and today both have an established jewelry context. The perceived value of materials is constantly changing, and new materials are constantly being reassessed. There are also those objects that do not fall so neatly into a jewelry context, yet they provoke thought and challenge our preconceptions, spelling out the function of details that we may otherwise take for granted. The use of screws in place of claws is one such example.

Found objects have also played a valuable role historically. Religious relics were, and still are, incorporated into jewelry forms as precious objects. Today, as our values change, the found object can be seen to reflect these changes. Its role as a natural resource keeps evolving beyond the predictable, and so we are constantly finding new relics to treasure.

A piece of meteorite is captured in a ring that tapers like a shooting star.

Traditionally, the materials associated with jewelry were metal—most often gold and silver—and precious and semiprecious stones. Other materials were generally used to imitate the real thing, but were not usually perceived as valuable in their own right. As jewelry has evolved, its preconcieved role as a bodily adornment displaying the wearer's wealth has changed into a more transient, expendable means of decoration. Through the use of new materials and modern methods of mechanized production, jewelry has become less costly, and is now commonly used to express or commemorate a tiny slice of time.

A gold leaf finish is visible through the plastic in this brooch.

Contemporary materials

Glass has been embedded into these stacked silver rings.

Contemporary materials often typify the decade in which they initially became popular. Bakelite was used in jewelry up to and during the 1950s, molded plastic made life brighter in the 1960s and 1970s, while during the 1980s you couldn't escape titanium jewelry—even you wanted to.

After the excesses of the boom-time 1980s, the 1990s saw the scale of jewelry shrink from the opulent to the modest, and reclaimed materials were often used to replace "space-age" titanium. As forms became more modest in size, materials considered spiritually uplifting or healing also saw an increase in popularity. Perceptions of jewelry have also changed, so that in affluent societies, where time can be devoted to culture and design, the intrinsic value of a material is no longer necessarily the primary reason for a purchase.

Today, there are very few materials that have not been tried in jewelry form. New ideas are increasingly valuable to an audience that is both design-conscious and intellectually curious. Many of today's designs use contemporary materials, wittily reversing the role and the preconceived value of a material or object. For example, a jewelry box can be made of a substance that is more valuable in material terms than the jewelry object that it contains.

Colored foil is laminated between sheets of Perspex to allow the iridescent color combination to radiate through.

A snakeskin effect is made from plastic in this shimmering pendant.

Gold leaf shines through this plastic necklace.

Some contemporary materials can be used in such a way that the material value of the piece is negligible, while its visual effect is substantial. For example, gold leaf can be used to back a plastic form, creating a piece with significant visual impact using a minimal amount of gold. Plastics can also be fashioned into sumptuous, tactile forms, or used to capture or accentuate iridescent colors. Although such metals as aluminum and titanium have little intrinsic value, they can be anodized to create bright, lustrous colors.

Contemporary materials change with time, with materials constantly gaining and losing contemporary status in jewelry terms. One example of an enduring material, however, is glass, which has been used in jewelry forms over the centuries. Today, broken fragments of modern safety glass are fashionably used in place of a stone, redefining it as a contemporary material and refreshing its image in a jewelry context.

In the realm of jewelry-making materials, "contemporary" is never a permanent title. Once a contemporary material has become established, it loses its contemporary status, and new materials will inevitably take over this title as they themselves become established in a jewelry context. The process of defining a material as contemporary is, however, of ongoing importance, as it ensures that the value and quality of materials are constantly being reevaluated. As long as this is done in conjunction with new ideas, and in keeping with overall quality, innovation in the realm of jewelry fabrication will continue to move forward.

Aluminum has been colored by anodizing in these brooches.

In this role reversal, a glass ring is contained inside a gold box.

Perspex is fashioned into beads that are alternately polished and frosted.

GLOSSARY

ANNEALING
The process of relieving stress within a metal by the application of heat. The temperature required to reach the point of annealing varies from one metal to another.

ANODIZING
A process for changing the surface color of metals using an electric current; commonly used for coloring aluminum and titanium.

ANTICLASTIC RAISING
A specialist raising technique that stretches metal sheet at the edges while compressing the center, thus allowing the sheet to bend in two opposing directions to create hollow, undulating forms.

BASE METAL
Non-precious metals such as copper, brass, gilding metal, nickel, pewter, steel, titanium, and aluminum.

BASSE-TAILLE
An enamelling technique in which the metal surface is engraved to different heights, thereby determining the color of transparent enamel.

BEZEL
A stone setting that uses a wall of metal to surround and set the stone.

BOLT RING
A catch that is circular in form that is used to secure necklaces, bracelets, and chains.

BRASS
A yellow-colored base metal.

BUTTERFLY BACK
An earring back used to secure an ear post, also known as a scroll back.

CABOCHON
The term used to describe a stone that has a smooth, rounded surface.

CASTING
A means of reproducing three-dimensional forms in metal. The metal is poured into a hollow form that can be made from a variety of media, including sand, cuttlefish, and plaster.

CHAMPLEVÉ
An enamelling technique that involves cutting chambers or cells in sheet, and then filling them with enamel.

CHANNEL SETTING
A stone-setting technique in which two walls of metal are formed like a gutter to hold in stones.

CHASING
A process of embossing the surface of sheet metal by hammering into it using steel tools.

CLAW SETTING
A setting in which prongs that resemble claws are used to hold a stone in place.

CLIPS
A type of earring fitting generally used for non-pierced ears.

CLOISONNÉ
An enamelling technique that involves making chambers or cells using wires on a metal sheet. The chambers or cells are then filled with enamel.

COPPER
A malleable red-colored base metal.

ELECTROFORMING
A process used to deposit a lightweight, hard skin of metal onto a form, partially or completely covering its surface.

ENAMELLING
A process for coloring jewelry by fusing a special type of glass to the surface of a metal.

ENGRAVING
The process of decorating metal by cutting away material using sharp steel tools called gravers.

ETCHING
The controlled corrosion of a surface using acids to create decorative or textured patterns.

FABRICATION
Construction from sheet and wire using hand tools.

FACETED
The term used to describe a cut stone.

FINISH
The final surface treatment of a piece.

FITTINGS
Hand-made components such as catches, joints, and clips.

FOIL
Thin silver or gold sheet that is slightly heavier than leaf; used in enamelling.

FORGING
A process in which metal is hammered in order to change its form.

FRETWORK
Sheet metal in which spaces have been cut away to make an ornamental lace-like pattern.

GEMSTONES
A term used to describe the precious and semiprecious stones used in jewelry.

GILDING
The process of gold-plating.

GILDING METAL
An alloy of copper that is well-suited to gilding.

GOLD
A precious metal traditionally used to make jewelry. In its purest form it is yellow, but it can also be alloyed to make white, red, or green colors.

GRAIN SETTING
A setting where a grain of metal is raised using a graver to set a stone.

GRANULATION
The use of tiny grains of silver or gold to decorate a surface.

GRAVER
A sharp steel tool used for engraving and setting.

GYPSY SETTING
A setting in which a stone is set into metal in such a way that it appears flush with the surface.

HINGE
A movable joint that turns or swings in a single plain, used to articulate two parts.

HOOK
A hook-shaped fitting for pierced earrings.

ILLUSION SETTING
A setting that is designed to enhance the appearance of a small stone, to make it seem larger.

INLAY
A process by which one metal is fused or soldered into another metal in a recess. The surface is then filed flush, so that the recessed material becomes clearly defined.

LATHE
A tool used for cutting a rotating object with accuracy.

LEAF
Thin sheet metal in silver and gold, used to create silver and gold surfaces. Imitation silver and gold leaf can also be found.

LINE JOINT
A means of linking that joins forms so that they appear in a line.

MILL PRESSING
A process for transferring a pattern or texture by passing sheet metal through rolling mills with paper or other materials.

MOHS SCALE
The Mohs scale is an indicator of the approximate relative hardness of stones based on their resistance to abrasion. The hardest—diamond—is rated 10, and the softest—talc—is rated 0.

MOKUMÉ GANE
A process in which layers of metal are fused together to make a mokumé laminate. A pattern is then created by etching, deforming, or cutting into the surface, then filing back and rolling flush the layers of metal exposed by the filing.

MALLEABILITY
In a jewelry context, this term describes metal that is pliable, meaning that it can be easily hammered, shaped, or pressed.

NICKEL
A silvery metal also known as nickel silver that is harder than copper and brass.

OMEGA CLIP
A non-pierced ear fitting that is shaped like the omega symbol.

OXIDIZING
A process for blackening metal using chemicals to create lowlights, giving the impression of aging.

PAINTING ENAMEL
An enamelling technique that involves painting with enamel paint on an opaque enamel surface (usually white).

PATINATION
A process for coloring metals by exposure to a variety of chemicals.

PAVÉ SETTING
A setting in which small stones of a similar size, usually round, are grain-set close together to cover an area, so that the area appears to be "paved" with stones.

PEWTER
A dark gray-colored tin-based metal.

PHOTOETCHING
A form of etching that uses ultraviolet light to expose artwork on sensitized metal sheets that are then etched.

PIERCING
Another term used to describe fretwork.

PIN
The wire with a sharpened end that is passed through fabric in order to fasten a brooch to a garment.

PLASTICS
Embedding and casting resins, Perspex sheet, and nylon are some of the plastics that are commonly used in jewelry-making.

PLATING
A fine covering of metal deposited on a metal surface by means of an electric current.

PLATINUM
A precious metal that is a darker gray color than silver, and approximately twice as heavy.

PLIQUE-À-JOUR
Plique-à-jour enamel has no backing, so that the enamelling can be viewed from both the front and the back.

POLISHED
A term used to describe a surface when it is cleaned of unwanted blemishes.

PRECIOUS
In the context of jewelry, this term is used to describe diamond, sapphire, emerald, and ruby stones, and gold, silver, and platinum metals.

PRESSING
A process by which hollow forms can be made.

RAISING
A process in which sheet metal is formed on steel forms called stakes to become three-dimensional.

REPOUSSÉ
The process of creating relief in sheet metal using steel tools that are hammered into metal from the back.

RETICULATION
A process that creates a web- or net-like effect on metal by the application of heat to the metal to a stage beyond annealed, but before melting, when the surface appears to "swim."

RIVET
A mechanical means of joining two or more parts by passing a pin through them. The ends of the pin are spread, so that it cannot come apart.

SCROLL BACK
An earring back used to secure an ear post, also known as a butterfly back.

SEMIPRECIOUS
In the context of jewelry, this term describes most of the stones that are used other than those that are precious.

SILVER
A light gray-colored precious metal that is traditionally used in jewelry-making.

SOLDERING
A process for joining metal using an alloy called solder that melts at a lower temperature than the metals it is used to join. When it cools, it forms a joint.

SPINNING
A process in which a disk of metal is eased over a solid, rotating form to create a hollow three-dimensional form.

STAKE
A steel form used for forming metal in raising and other techniques.

STEEL
A hard, dark gray-colored base metal that is often used for making tools.

SWIVEL FITTING
A type of fitting that is used for securing necklaces and bracelets.

SYNTHETIC STONES
Stones that are manufactured to simulate precious and semiprecious stones.

TENSION SETTING
A type of setting that relies on the strength of metal to support and hold a stone in place by tension on two sides.

TEXTURE
A visual or tactile surface given to a form.

INDEX